A Creative Strategy for Assuring Success

A CREATIVE STRATEGY FOR ASSURING SUCCESS

A Model for Facilitating Effective Cross-Cultural Mentoring

Alfred H. McPherson, MSW

VANTAGE PRESS
New York

FIRST EDITION

Published by Vantage Press, Inc.
516 West 34th Street, New York, New York 10001

Manufactured in the United States of America
ISBN: 0-533-09443-7

Library of Congress Catalog Card No.: 90-90451

0 9 8 7 6 5 4 3 2 1

To the memory of my mother, Lucille,
and
to my beloved wife, Gwendolyin,
and daughter, Kimberly

CONTENTS

INTRODUCTION

PART I

This book is specifically designed to promote the development of human effectiveness in interpersonal relationships. It is recommended to anyone who is interested in fully developing his potential or working with others who need to develop theirs. It evolved from the personal experiences of the author in working with thousands of persons from a variety of social and economic backgrounds.

The concepts are in wide use in a number of educational, correctional, and business institutions. Many of its concepts have been repeatedly validated through research by a number of creditable sources.

Research has indicated that even successful people only use about 10 to 15 percent of their potential. Therefore, most of us can achieve significantly beyond whatever level we happen to be performing.

This book will help build your confidence, increase your decision-making ability, help you understand yourself and others better, and provide you with a number of strategies that have a proven track record in motivating others to achieve. It will make you a more effective mentor.

Part I focuses upon dealing with certain assumptions about human behavior and the implications of those assumptions. The primary purpose of Part I is to provide an overview of the issues that have a significant impact on effective human functioning.

PART II

Part II focuses upon problem solving and self-awareness. It introduces a specific model for making more effective decisions. It also has an insightful model for expanding your awareness of personal strengths and weaknesses, many of which you might not be aware. It will sharpen your ability to deal objectively with issues which may be of a personal nature. In addition, it will help you to approach problems and crises in a rational manner. It will also help you deal more effectively with irrational feelings and behaviors.

Part II also introduces the B-D Scale. The B-D Scale is a self-awareness model designed to help a person see beyond the defense mechanism he erects to protect himself from his own inadequacies. The B-D Scale graphically defines success and failure in terms easy to understand and apply. It shows how a person becomes acclimated to failure during his formative years and how early negative conditioning makes it difficult for this person to succeed in later years. It also identifies critical factors which mitigate against a person's becoming successful. It shows how a person can be programmed to succeed. There are various exercises to help you determine whether you were programmed to succeed or fail and where you stand in relationship to the rest of society.

PART III

Part III deals with fifteen human needs, suggesting options, alternatives, and consequences that can be associated with each specific need area.

PART IV

Part IV is structured to provide a number of strategies that may be utilized effectively to deal with a variety of essential human needs.

A Creative Strategy for Assuring Success

PART I

Common Assumptions about Human Behavior

INTRODUCTORY EXERCISE

This introductory exercise is an important first step. It will sharpen your focus upon ideas and issues which might mitigate against your maximizing your potential. Your answers reflect your personal philosophy. Your philosophy affects your decision making. Your decision making produces consequences.

* * * *

The following are a set of assumptions about human behavior and development. If you agree with the assumption, check *True*. If you disagree, check *False*. If you have doubts, check *Maybe*.

	True	False	Maybe
1. Every individual is entitled to dignity and respect.	_____	_____	_____
2. Everyone's feelings and viewpoint should be respected.	_____	_____	_____
3. The most critical developmental period in a person's life occurs before age five.	_____	_____	_____
4. Generally, people who fail feel they cannot control their own lives.	_____	_____	_____
5. It is difficult for a person to fail and not know it.	_____	_____	_____
6. No one likes to fail—they just become used to it.	_____	_____	_____
7. The best way to help a person who is failing is to tell him about his problem.	_____	_____	_____
8. Everyone is aware of when they are being successful.	_____	_____	_____
9. People who know better tend to do better.	_____	_____	_____
10. People often fail because they are programmed to fail by their society or environment.	_____	_____	_____

	True	False	Maybe
11. People often succeed because they are programmed to succeed by their society or environment.	_____	_____	_____
12. The first step toward success is recognition of the need for change.	_____	_____	_____
13. Peer pressure helps to modify individual behavior.	_____	_____	_____
14. People will change if they feel it is in their best interest.	_____	_____	_____
15. Everyone knows how to think critically.	_____	_____	_____
16. Self-esteem is critical in the learning process.	_____	_____	_____
17. Low self-esteem adversely affects motivation.	_____	_____	_____
18. It is easier to change behavior than it is to change values.	_____	_____	_____
19. There is no such thing as a "little" success.	_____	_____	_____
20. The truth is what a person believes it is.	_____	_____	_____

Now that you have completed this exercise, carefully review your response to each statement before checking your response against those outlined in "Common Assumptions Regarding Human Behavior Inventory."

COMMON ASSUMPTIONS REGARDING HUMAN BEHAVIOR INVENTORY

Success is a journey, not a destination. However, many people perceive success to be just that: a destination. These people have difficulty with appreciating even modest achievements. Others tend to feel that anyone can be successful if only he is properly motivated.

This book debunks many of these assumptions. The author feels that success is a learned and programmed process and that it is not just the product of conscious will or simple platitudes. People succeed when they are programmed to do so. Likewise, people fail when they are not programmed to succeed.

The author will explain twenty common assumptions about human behavior and provide some insight into how our behavior is affected by them.

ASSUMPTION #1—Every individual is entitled to dignity and respect.

The correct answer is *False*. Some people believe this statement to be true. They feel that dignity and respect are entitlements that naturally accrue to one who happens to be a member of the human race. However, they fail to see that both **dignity** and **respect** are only accorded to the person who **earns** it, and even then, it may not be accorded. When people understand that dignity and respect are not entitlements but are by-products of conscious action, they greatly increase the likelihood of being accorded both.

ASSUMPTION #2—Everyone's feelings and viewpoints should be respected.

The correct answer is *False*. A large number of people believe this statement to be true. They feel that regardless of how you feel about another person's feelings and viewpoints, you should respect them. In reality, most of us can easily think of a number of people whose feelings and viewpoints are not respected by us, nor do we feel compelled to do so. People are free to choose what they want to feel and believe, but they are not protected from the penalties which occur when those feelings and viewpoints are out of step with the times or their peers.

ASSUMPTION #3—The most critical developmental period in a person's life occurs before age five.

The correct answer is *True*. Many people feel otherwise. They think that the late teens or middle years are the most critical period. However, a number of studies emanating from research on Headstart preschool programs tend to indicate that the preschool era is the most critical in setting the stage for future development and success later in life. During this period the person learns how to walk, talk, and manipulate his environment. These skills set the pace for how the person will respond to a wider society. The person's personality is also highly developed during the first five years.

ASSUMPTION #4—Generally, people who fail feel they cannot control their own lives.

The correct answer is *True*. However, many people believe that statement to be false. They say that people who fail look for reasons to explain their failures. Few people enjoy the consequences of failure. Therefore, it is incumbent upon them to develop a sound rationale to explain the failure. This process usually involves seeking and identifying outside forces over which the person who failed had no control. This absolves the person of any blame for the outcome, because the outside forces were unpredictable and were beyond the person's control. Put more simply, no one likes to do something stupid and acknowledge it. When a person confronts the part he personally played in the failure, he immediately begins turning things around.

ASSUMPTION #5—It is difficult for a person to fail and not know it.

The correct answer is *False*. Some people believe this assumption to be true. They tend to feel that everyone is aware of when they are failing. These people tend to feel that failure is so obvious that it is easily perceived by any rational person. What these people fail to see is that because failure tends to produce negative consequences, it makes many people so defensive, they deny its existence or they redefine the consequences until they become respectable. For example, a fisherman who loses a big fish will have difficulty in recounting the experience without elaborating or fictionalizing the event.

Denial of failure is a common coping mechanism. It allows a person to continue failing without having to accept responsibility. The more he does it, the easier it becomes.

ASSUMPTION #6—No one likes to fail—they just become used to it.

The correct answer is *False*. Many people believe this statement to be true. They feel that it is not possible for anyone to like failure. They are appalled that people can accept failure. What they fail to see, partly because they don't want to and because it is foreign to their personal experience and education, is that many people have adjusted to failure and accept it as a way of life. They expect the worst, and they get it. They have extreme difficulty dealing with success. For example, one of the common perceptions of an avowed failure is: "If I didn't have bad luck, I wouldn't have any luck at all." Many criminals brag about how many times they have been caught and imprisoned, not about how many times they got away. People who like failure have accepted it as a way of life, and sometimes they take pride in it. They experience no anxiety when they fail. They rationalize failure and resign themselves to the outcome. They often feel that if they **tried** to succeed, no one can blame them for failing. **Trying** becomes the **key** which absolves them of guilt or responsibility for their failure.

ASSUMPTION #7—The best way to help a person who is failing is to tell him about his problem.

The correct answer is *False*. Many people believe this statement to be true. They feel that the best way to help a person is to tell him about his problem. What they fail to see, however, is that it is one of the worst ways to help a person, because usually when we tell someone about his problem, it is because it is causing us some concern. When that happens, how objective are we in our feedback? We are not. In many cases we do not have all of the facts. The best way to help a person is not to tell him about his problem, but assist him in developing viable alternatives. People tend to respond more positively when provided with solutions as opposed to having their problems delineated. It is important that the person with the problem **seek** help from others. If this is not done, then you might be able to help him by calling the problem to his attention. However, by no stretch of the imagination is this the best way to help a person you think is having a problem.

ASSUMPTION #8—Everyone is aware of when they are being successful.

The correct answer is *False*. Many people believe this statement to be true. They feel that success is such an obvious thing that it is inconceivable that one could have it and not know. Yet even these people know personally someone who has refused to believe that he is successful. This statement is false, because many people who are successful do not perceive themselves to be successful. Many people are apologetic for their success. They feel they are unworthy of it. Many are embarrassed by their achievements. They downplay their accomplishments, and they wish others would do likewise. Generally these people probably will never enjoy their success. They think of success as a destination. They feel they haven't arrived at that point. Unfortunately, many of them will go through life feeling inadequate and unfulfilled.

ASSUMPTION #9—People who know better tend to do better.

The correct answer is *True*. Many people when confronted with this assumption believe it to be false. They feel that knowing better does not necessarily make one do better. However, they overlook the key word in the statement. That word is **"tend."** It does not mean that a person would do better, but that there is a tendency for the person to do better. For example, a person who is exceeding the speed limit and is unaware of it has no guilt about breaking the law, but a person who is aware of the speed limit feels guilt when he exceeds it, and that guilt tends to influence his behavior. Therefore, knowledge has its own value. It is much more difficult to do something stupid when one knows better. People tend to believe that they cannot be held responsible for something of which they had no prior knowledge.

ASSUMPTION #10—People often fail because they are programmed to fail by their society or environment.

The correct answer is *True*. Society determines who will fail through cultural and economic determinants. Many people tend to believe that failing is more a product of personal choice as opposed to external factors. Society sets the rules, values, and sanctions. The expectations of society serve as a yardstick for measuring performance. Most societies are designed to ensure that some members will be advantaged and others will be disadvantaged. Both groups adapt successfully to their prescribed roles. Therefore, it is clear that failure is no accident, but is a product of conscious intervention by the decision makers who control a given society. People tend to fail because of their inability to cope effectively with the following factors:

F rustration
A nger
I nsecurity
L oneliness
U ncertainty
R esentment
E nvy

Frustration usually results from a lot of unmet needs. Generally a person who fails feels that he lacks adequate resources. In short, he feels he never has enough of anything. He tends to feel that the world is against him.

Anger is a by-product of frustration. The person feels uptight because things are not going the way he feels they should. Many times the anger is too sharp for the person to control. This is one of the reasons many people who are angry turn to alcohol or drugs. They feel it will make them feel and perform better than they would have had they not used the drug or alcohol.

Insecurity is a key factor in failing. The person is very unsure of himself. The person lacks confidence in his judgment. Because of prior poor decisions, the person feels incompetent. Therefore, any decision he makes is likely to produce negative consequences.

Loneliness is the result of past failure. People tend to avoid people that fail. So a frustrated, angry, insecure person is likely to be avoided by others. His isolation only increases his frustration, anger, and insecurity.

Uncertainty is a by-product of frustration, anger, insecurity, and loneliness. The person tends to live one day at a time. He loses confidence in the future. He becomes survivor-oriented. He loses faith in tomorrow. He is afraid to deal with long-range goals. He tends to view life as a an ordeal one must overcome.

Resentment evolves from the perception that things are bad, they have always been bad, and they are not going to get any better. The person tends to feel that the **"deck"** is stacked against him. Any success enjoyed by others tends to magnify his failure and fuel his resentment.

Envy occurs when the person is confronted with a successful peer. The person who is failure-oriented has that failure illuminated when encountering a successful peer. He tends to feel that his peer's success is a result more of luck than of effort or talent, that the only difference between his failure and his peer's success is luck.

ASSUMPTION #11—People often succeed because they are programmed to succeed by their society or environment.

The correct answer is *True*. Like failure, success is not an accident. People succeed when they are programmed to succeed. A lot of people like to take all the credit for their success. They tend to discount the value of the role their parents and others played in their success. Of course, not all people programmed to succeed will succeed, but the vast majority will. Successful parents usually raise successful children. People who are programmed to succeed are generally indoctrinated with the following values:

S ense of Direction
U nderstanding
C ourage
C harity
E mpathy
S elf-acceptance
S elf-confidence

Sense of Direction is extremely important in the success process. A person programmed to succeed is taught goal-setting very early in his personal development. He is also taught who he is and what he can become.

Understanding is another key factor acquired by a person programmed to succeed. Not only is he taught goals, but he is also taught to understand what is required. It is great to have a goal, but it is equally important to understand what it costs. Planning, execution, commitment, and perseverance require considerable understanding.

Courage is one of the most important values instilled in a person programmed to succeed. Success requires the courage to fail. A person programmed to succeed views failure as a challenge rather than as a consequence. He is undaunted by failure because it is perceived as a temporary setback and a prerequisite for any worthwhile challenge.

Charity is an integral part of success programming. People aren't born charitable. It is a learned value. People who are programmed for success are taught very early in their development the value of charity. They are taught that it is their duty to help those less fortunate than themselves. A person programmed to fail tends to view charity as his just reward. He believes it is better to receive than it is to give.

Empathy is a key ingredient in success programming. The ability and willingness to have an open mind, to look at a situation from the other person's point of view, to compromise, and to consider the possibility that one might be wrong is an incalculable value. A person programmed to fail usually only looks at one side, his own.

Self-acceptance is critical in successfully programming a person to succeed. A person has to believe in himself. A person is taught to accept himself by the actions of others as opposed to words. A person programmed to succeed is not only **taught** that he is important, but he is **treated** as though he is important. Generally a person who is programmed to fail is often made to feel that he is unworthy. He tends to confuse rejection of certain types of behavior as a rejection of himself. People programmed to succeed are taught that the rejection of certain behaviors must not be perceived as a rejection of the person.

Self-confidence comes with achievement. The more achievement a person has, the greater the self-confidence. When a person is programmed to succeed, he is deliberately given challenges congruent with his abilities, aptitudes, and interests. Adequate support is given to assure success. Although failure is not eradicated, it is minimized and controlled.

ASSUMPTION #12—The first step toward success is recognition of the need for change.

The correct answer is *True*. Whenever a person becomes aware of a need for change, he has, although inadvertently, initiated the change process. The fact that better alternatives exist becomes a powerful force for change. The insight of options creates a desire for change. The new insight creates discomfort for the status quo, so even if a person doesn't change, he does not enjoy the old status as much.

ASSUMPTION #13—Peer pressure helps to modify individual behaviors.

The correct answer is *True*. Regardless of what we think of the Joneses, when they buy a new car, it hurts. Our old car suddenly is no longer acceptable. There is no comparison. All of us are affected by peer pressure either positively or negatively. Rarely are we neutral.

ASSUMPTION #14—People will change if they feel it is in their best interest.

The correct answer is *Maybe*. Sometimes they will and sometimes they won't. Sometimes people are aware of behaviors detrimental to their personal welfare, but they continue the activity. Others, however, become aware and immediately change their behavior.

ASSUMPTION #15—Everyone knows how to think critically.

The correct answer is *False*. Some people cannot think themselves out of a single room with four exit signs. They can never decide upon which exit to use. Yet many people tend to endow everyone with "common sense" or the ability to make rational decisions. Unfortunately, the ability to think critically was not universally bestowed upon the human race. Most people can significantly increase their cognitive skills through education and training.

ASSUMPTION #16—Self-esteem is critical in the learning process.

The correct answer is *True*. How a person feels about himself is key in the learning process. The better a person feels about himself, the better he feels about new challenges. Since most learning requires interaction with others, the more effective the interaction, the greater the opportunity for acquiring new knowledge and skills. One of the reasons people fail is because of low self-esteem and deficient social interaction skills.

ASSUMPTION #17—Low self-esteem adversely affects motivation.

The correct answer is *True*. Low self-esteem lowers initiative. The person with low self-esteem tends to avoid challenges which might validate his inadequacies. He tends to become more inner directed than outer directed. He tends to avoid even minimal challenges and appears to be disinterested in activities common among his peers.

ASSUMPTION #18—It is easier to change behavior than it is to change values.

The correct answer is *True*. Behavioral change is easier to produce because it is not diffused or deeply entrenched, as values are. In fact, it is easy for one to behave counter to what he feels or believes. For example, during wartime many are taught how to kill other human beings and they do so even though they are personally against the taking of human life.

ASSUMPTION #19—There is no such thing as a little success.

The correct answer is *True*. Success should not be broken down into pieces. To do so devalues success. People who tend not to believe the above statement have a tendency of downplaying achievement. They do not feel successful unless they perform substantially above what is reasonably expected. They also tend to view success as an outcome or destination rather than as a journey. It is not a **point** a person arrives at, but it is the **process** of traveling.

ASSUMPTION #20—The truth is what a person believes it to be.

The correct answer is *True*. Many people tend to think that there is "*the truth*" rather than "*a truth.*" They are correct. However, many believe that the truth is what a person believes it is. They are also correct. Truth is a very personal value. It gets its validity from the individual. The person is the sole validating agent of truth. So if a person believes this statement to be false, he would also be correct, because he is the prime validating agent for discerning "*truths.*"

PART II

Problem Solving and Self-Awareness

DECISION-MAKING PROCESS

This is a specialized process which can be used to help you become a better decision maker. It is outlined in a series of steps listed chronologically in terms of sequence and importance.

Step 1

Define the word *THINK*. Take a pen and paper and write the definition down without looking up the word in a dictionary. After you are satisfied with your definition, move on to step 2.

Step 2

Define the word *REASON*. Again, please do so without looking up the definition. Once you are satisfied with your definition, move on to step 3.

Step 3

Define the word *KNOWLEDGE*. Do not use a dictionary. Use your familiarity with the concept to develop your personal definition. Move on to step 4 after you develop a definition with which you are satisfied.

Step 4

Divide knowledge into two bodies of information. The first body will be known as *empirical* knowledge. Write down your idea of what you think *empirical* knowledge is. After you are satisfied with your answer, move on to the next body of knowledge, which is called *metaphysical*. Again write your definition of what you think *metaphysical* knowledge is.

If you did not cheat by using a dictionary, the chances are you had a very difficult time completing steps 1–4. In fact, there is a good possibility that you could not get beyond step 3. Don't feel bad. Why is it so difficult?

The answer is simple. The vast majority of people do not understand what metaphysical and empirical knowledge is comprised of. So again, if you missed these steps, you have something in common with millions of people. In order to effectively complete the exercise outlined, you had to first *think*—that is, you had to use your mind. Since thinking is an abstract process, it is exceedingly difficult to define. However, the broader our definition, the broader the utility. The more familiar one is with the process, the easier and more effective he is in utilizing it. The less familiarity, the more difficulty he will encounter. The ability to *think* makes it easier for you to *reason.* Thinking allows you to more effectively assess cause and effect. You are better able to compare and weigh information. Therefore, the ability to *reason* requires the ability to *think.*

Once we begin to *think* and *reason*, we create a by-product called *knowledge*, which can be defined as a sum total of a person's life experience at any given point or time. Knowledge can be effectively broken down into two major bodies of information: *empirical* and *metaphysical.* Empirical knowledge is the body of information that can be ascertained extrinsically. That is, it exists in what we commonly call the *real* world or *objective* world. It has size, shape, bulk, and form that can be externally validated by independent research. All empirical data must be validated externally.

Metaphysical knowledge is that body of information that is validated intrinsically. That is, its validity is contingent upon an individual's perception. It is known as the *ideal* world. It is comprised of feelings, religion, politics, values, truth, color, et cetera. *Metaphysical* knowledge cannot exist unless it is internally validated by the individual. You might ask, "What does all of this really mean? How does it affect me, if at all?" First let me say that it affects all of us very much. For example, whenever a person fails at a particular task, he looks for ways to establish why he did not succeed. However, he does not look internally for the answer. He looks externally. When he can identify externally the factors he feels are responsible for his failure, he is no longer compelled to take responsibility for his failure. He is able to effectively shift blame from himself to factors over which he has no control. Since he does this subconsciously, he is not consciously aware that he is fooling himself! Therefore, there is a tendency for all of us to subconsciously blame others for failure which rightfully belongs to us.

The following exercise will help you understand the difference between metaphysical statements and empirical statements. Please check what you believe is the best answer for each of the ten statements listed.

	True	False
1. The truth can be anything you want it to be.	_____	_____
2. People tend to respond more to beliefs than to facts.	_____	_____
3. People are always aware of when they are lying.	_____	_____
4. People tend to make their decisions based upon facts.	_____	_____
5. It is easy to change a person's mind by presenting him with the facts.	_____	_____
6. Everyone knows the difference between right and wrong, because all it takes is common sense.	_____	_____
7. It is easier to make a decision based on beliefs than it is to make one based on facts.	_____	_____
8. Facts often threaten one's beliefs.	_____	_____
9. It is okay for someone to make a mistake, if he believed he was doing the right thing.	_____	_____
10. Anger does not really affect the quality of one's decision.	_____	_____

Carefully review your answers before reviewing the answers which follow.

Answer to #1: *True*. Rationale: All truth is metaphysical and it is validated by the individual.

Answer to #2: *True*. Rationale: Beliefs are far more powerful motivators than are facts. Facts tend to be relevant only when they are supportive of the belief.

Answer to #3: *False*. Rationale: Lying is metaphysical; therefore, it is not unusual for a person to often be unaware of his own lies on a conscious level.

Answer to #4: *False*. Rationale: Facts do not motivate. How one *feels* about the facts becomes the principal motivation.

Answer to #5: *False*. Rationale: Facts do not motivate most people to change their minds if the facts are counter to what the person really wants to believe. Accepting the facts forces the person to alter his belief, and that is not easy to do.

Answer to #6: *False.* Rationale: It takes more than common sense to discern the difference between right and wrong, because both are metaphysical and they require more than common sense to unravel.

Answer to #7: *True.* Rationale: Beliefs are metaphysical and personal. We feel great about making decisions which are congruent with our feelings.

Answer to #8: *True.* Rationale: Facts are cold and impersonal. They are not interested in taking sides. They stand alone. Beliefs are personal. They are predicated upon one's feeling. Often it is difficult to articulate what we feel, let alone be able to prove it.

Answer to #9: *False.* Rationale: It is not okay for someone to make a mistake even if he believed he was doing the right thing. Believing does not make a person less responsible for his actions.

Answer to #10: *False.* Rationale: Anger plays a significant role in altering our perceptions. Therefore, it would greatly influence the quality of any decision made while the person was angry.

* * * *

This next exercise is designed to help you recognize empirical and metaphysical statements and their implications. Remember that all empirical statements must be externally provable. Circle *M* if you believe the statement to be **metaphysical**, or *E* if you feel the statement is **empirical**.

1. My feet hurt.	M	E
2. I saw John hit Bill with the hammer.	M	E
3. If you walk in front of a car, you will be killed.	M	E
4. Mary is truly a beautiful woman.	M	E
5. The sun rises and sets each day.	M	E
6. Truth and facts are both the same.	M	E
7. If you want success, you must work hard.	M	E
8. Metal is used to make appliances.	M	E
9. There are twelve months in a calendar year.	M	E
10. Police officers are hired to protect the public.	M	E

11. People carry guns to protect themselves. M E
12. If I play the lottery, I have a good chance of winning. M E
13. The state is the real winner of the state lottery. M E
14. Haste makes waste. M E
15. You can't hurt what you love. M E
16. Politics are generally based on a set of beliefs. M E
17. Everyone believes in God. M E
18. The United States is comprised of fifty-two states. M E
19. I am what I think I am. M E
20. People usually die before reaching their one hundredth birthday. M E

Now check your responses against the answers which follow:

Answer to #1: *M*. Rationale: There is no way you can empirically prove that your feet hurt. It is real only to you. However, you can prove that your foot is broken or injured, because evidence would be there to prove it extrinsically.

Answer to #2: *E*. Rationale: You can empirically prove or disprove whether or not John hit Bill with the hammer because ample physical evidence exists.

Answer to #3: *M*. Rationale: The car may not even be moving. This is only an opinion expressed, and opinions are metaphysical.

Answer to #4: *M*. Rationale: Beauty is in the eye of the beholder. It merely represents a person's personal opinion.

Answer to #5: *E*. Rationale: Empirical data exist which predict the sunrise and the sunset.

Answer to #6: *M*. Rationale: Truth and facts are not the same. Truth is metaphysical, and facts are empirical. Truth is also an opinion, and opinions cannot be validated externally.

Answer to #7: *M*. Rationale: This statement merely expresses an opinion and cannot be validated externally.

Answer to #8: *E*. Rationale: This statement is empirical, because it can be validated externally.

Answer to #9: *E*. Rationale: Physical evidence exists to either prove or disprove this statement, therefore, it can be validated externally.

Answer to #10: *M*. Rationale: This statement merely expresses an opinion which cannot be empirically substantiated.

Answer to #11: *M*. Rationale: This statement cannot be empirically proven, therefore, it cannot be validated externally.

Answer to #12: *M*. Rationale: This statement merely expresses an opinion which cannot be empirically proven.

Answer to #13: *M*. Rationale: This statement is a value judgment which cannot be empirically substantiated.

Answer to #14: *M*. Rationale: This statement is simply an opinion which cannot validated or substantiated empirically.

Answer to #15: *M*. Rationale: This statement is a value judgment which expresses an opinion or wish, but it cannot be externally validated.

Answer to #16: *E*. Rationale: It can be objectively proven that politics is based on a set of beliefs because the beliefs are identifiable and can be empirically validated or invalidated.

Answer to #17: *M*. Rationale: This statement cannot be empirically proven. It merely expresses an opinion that cannot be validated externally.

Answer to #18: *E*. Rationale: This statement is empirical even though it can be disproved empirically. Therefore, it can be externally validated or invalidated.

Answer to #19: *M*. Rationale: This statement merely expresses an opinion which cannot be empirically proven.

Answer to #20: *E*. Rationale: This statement is empirical, because it is a statement which can be externally validated or invalidated.

Read over this exercise until you get a full understanding of how to apply the concepts. Remember the application of these concepts requires that you **think**, **reason**, and carefully expand your **knowledge** base. The results will be remarkable.

THE B-D SCALE

The B-D Scale is an exciting tool to expand and broaden a person's knowledge of himself and others. It was initially designed to assist people who were exposed to failure over a prolonged period and who had reached a point where they no longer dreaded failure but found it to be compatible. The results were outstanding. Thousands of people have been exposed to these concepts, and many credit them with improving their lives immeasurably. The B-D Scale was developed by the author to break down the defense mechanisms that all of us erect to protect us from our own inadequacies. So prepare yourself for a unique and exciting journey. The decision-making process you just completed will help you understand and utilize the insights you garner from the B-D Scale.

* * * *

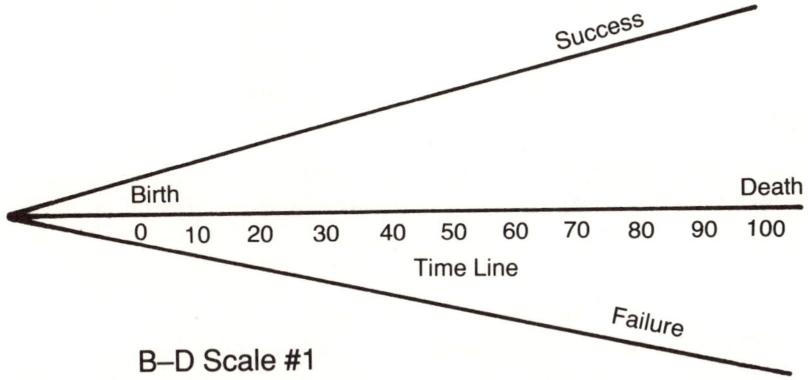

B–D Scale #1

The B-D Scale is pictured above. The scale is developed by identifying the **two** most **significant** events which occur during a lifetime. These two events are **birth** and **death**. No two events are more significant than when a person enters the world and when he leaves. Once born, a person must stay here until death occurs. In other words, there is only one way in and only one way out. During those two periods a lot of things occur. Collectively they determine whether the person will succeed or fail. The B-D Scale has a success line, time line, and failure line. When we say a person is succeeding in the world, we generally think of him as going up. When we say a person is failing, we generally perceive him as going down. Therefore, those two lines represent our ups and downs. The time line represents our life span. It is depicted in increments of ten up to one hundred years. It stops there because by that time the majority of us are no longer around. There are five factors which play a major role in determining whether a person succeeds or fails on the B-D Scale. These factors are:

1. AREA OR ENVIRONMENT

If the environment is a positive one—that is, if it provides the person with advantages—it helps to set the person up for success. However, if the situation happens to be negative, it tends to set the person up for failure.

2. HEALTH

The health of the person at birth is key in helping to determine whether the person is programmed to succeed or fail. This includes both physical and mental health.

3. WEALTH

Wealth is the third key factor. The wealth or lack of it is a big predeterminer of whether a person is programmed to succeed or fail.

4. SEX

We are talking gender, not sex. Whether a person is male or female is extremely important in determining success options.

5. RACE

Even though much progress has been made, race is still a potent predictor of success or failure a person is likely to experience on the B-D Scale.

The five factors listed above interact together to determine the level of success or failure the person will more than likely encounter. In addition to these five factors, another significant factor emerges which has a strong and decisive role to play in determining the extent to which a person is likely to fail or succeed. This factor is the **formative years** of the person, commonly considered the first five years after birth. It is during this period that the personality is developed. This is also the period during which the person develops the key coping skills that will pave the way for the success the person will encounter later. If this period was positive, meaning that the coping skills developed by the person were more than adequate to permit him to effectively apply them later on, the person is considered programmed to succeed. However, if this period was negative, meaning that the person's coping skills were undeveloped or poorly developed, then that person is considered as being programmed to fail. Research tends to show that persons programmed to fail during their formative years will more than likely fail in later years. It also shows that persons programmed to succeed during their formative years will more than likely succeed in later years. Keep this information in mind as you pursue an understanding of the B-D Scale. Once a person is programmed to succeed or fail, this program is usually maintained throughout the lifetime of the person. In fact, much of our government's policy today recognizes this and as a result, more and more dollars are being directed toward preschool and elementary students. The goal is to program the person to succeed as early as possible in life.

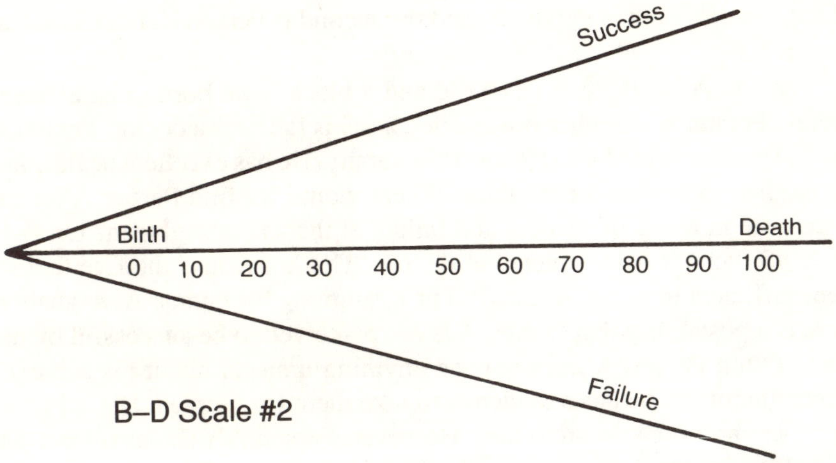

B–D Scale #2

Critical Factors

1. Area or Environment
2. Health
3. Wealth
4. Sex
5. Race

Key formative years—birth to 5 years of age.

Figure 1

CRITICAL FACTORS

In our society usually a person is given the opportunity to control and direct his own life by the age of eighteen. Some do it earlier, others later, and some never assume control. Figure 1 identifies the five critical factors, plus the key formative years that set the stage for success or failure.

In B-D Scale #3 pictured on page 25, two new elements have been added. One element is Person A, and the second is Person B. Let us look at Person A first.

Person A is eighteen years old and a black male born in an affluent suburb. Person A's mother is a teacher, and his father is a doctor. Person A has just been accepted into Howard University. He has excellent health, and his mother and father are wealthy. Where would we find Person A on the B-D Scale in terms of success and failure at the age of eighteen? On B-D Scale #3, Person A is depicted at the top. That's because the five factors were sufficient to ensure successful programming for Person A. Arguably, there is a possibility that Person A is not perceived to be successful by his peers. Often Person A does not see anything unusual about his achievements; therefore, he has a tendency to take them for granted. His achievements are nothing special to him. However, Person A's achievements are lauded by his parents, because for the first eighteen years Person A's success was, in fact, the parents' success. It should also be noted that most people reviewing Person A's circumstances would have difficulty believing that Person A did not, at eighteen, generally perceive himself as being successful. One reason for that is that when something appears to be obvious to us, then we presume it to be equally obvious to everyone else, especially the one who happens to be the prime beneficiary. Person A had been programmed to succeed, but in many instances, such a person is unaware of this. Person A might not succeed. However, the odds are heavily in Person A's favor.

How about Person B? Is Person B at a disadvantage? Now let's take a look at Person B. Person B is eighteen years old and a black male born in a very poor, crime-ridden neighborhood. Person B's mother has twelve children. She is unmarried and does not know who Person B's father is. Person B dropped out of school early, is unemployed, and is serving two years' probation. If we look at B-D Scale #3, we can readily discern that Person B is on the bottom of the B-D Scale.

Does either Person A, who is programmed to succeed, or Person B,

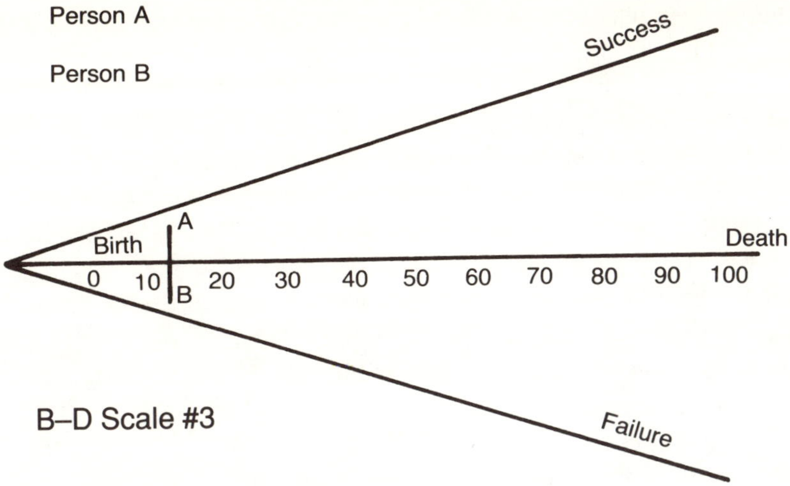

B–D Scale #3

who is programmed to fail, view himself as being successful or failing? The answer is a resounding **"no."** Neither Person A nor Person B perceives himself as successful or failing. Person A does not consider himself successful for a number of key reasons, the first being Person A evaluates himself in terms of his peers. Since his behavior is on par with that of his peers, he sees nothing special about his relative position. Person B does not evaluate his success in terms of Person A. He evaluates himself in terms of his peers. Since in many instances Person B is no worse off than most of his peers, he tends to feel pretty good about his position on the B-D Scale, which happens to be at the bottom. If Person B is outperforming his peers, then he considers himself a success. So in essence, what we have here is a situation where Person A is programmed to succeed and doesn't know it and Person B is programmed to fail and doesn't know it. What are generally the consequences of such perceptions? Person A was programmed to succeed upon conception. Person A more than likely received excellent prenatal care, was born in a good hospital, and came home to a bedroom specifically designed for his comfort. He received prompt medical attention to detect any possible deficiencies which might affect his chances for success later in life.

How about Person B? He was programmed to fail upon conception. In many cases, his was an unwanted birth. Many times such a baby receives little or no prenatal care. He does not normally come home to a room especially prepared for his comfort. He seldom gets adequate medical attention even when the problem is obvious. He learns quickly to survive. The attitudes and values he developed during his formative years substantially reduce his prospects for success later in life. So what will more than likely happen to Person B? He will become truant and defiant, drop out of school early, start smoking and drinking, defy authority, and experience juvenile detention, prison, and ultimately an early and untimely death.

Can Person B be helped? The answer is "yes," but . . . There are many buts, because a lot of things have to happen first. Person B has to first recognize that he has a problem. Person B does not perceive himself as a failure regardless of his long list of failures. The next step involves doing something about what he really sees of himself. This is not easy, because it is difficult to overcome years of negative conditioning. The B-D Scale provides both Person A and Person B the opportunity to graphically assess their positions in society and provides an opportunity for both to use that knowledge to further their personal growth and development.

Like Person B, Person A is sometimes victimized by his successful programming by his parents. Many times Person A will reject his success programming, because he feels his parents are controlling and directing his life. He rebels and sometimes totally rejects his successful life script. So he too, even though he has been programmed to succeed, fails to appreciate the intention of his parents.

Person B accepts his negative programming but tends to blame his parents for his predicament. He becomes survival-oriented and generally ends up going through life as a marginal performer, greatly wasting his talents and potential.

In the beginning of this book, I identified the success and failure characteristics which can help you better understand Person B and Person A's programming. There are four basic positions on the B-D Scale. See below.

Position #1 is a position whereby the person has high ideals but is in reality functioning on the bottom of the B-D Scale. The "M" stands for the metaphysical or **idealized** position. The "E" stands for the empirical or **real** level on which the person is functioning. Position #1 is a very poor position, because the distance between where the person sees himself someday being and where he is, in fact, functioning at present is too great. Therefore, it is highly unlikely the person at position #1 will ever achieve his idealized goal. The peers of the person at position #1 are probably not aspiring to the same heights as he is. That would tend to indicate that the person has considerably more potential than his peers, therefore, because of his superior potential he tends to enjoy the benefits of success without having to pay the price of success. His peers know that he has the potential to leave them, but that he would rather waste his potential than separate himself from them.

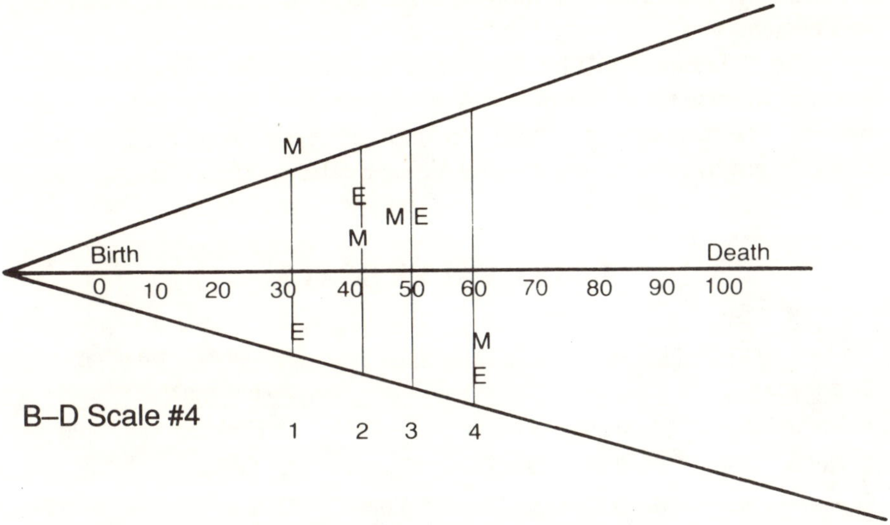

B–D Scale #4

Position #2, where the M is over the E, is indicative of a high achiever with a low self-concept. He has achieved more than he felt himself capable of, therefore, he is experiencing anxiety about his success. It is a typical successful female or black male position, because generally women and black males are expected to only go so high and in a limited number of occupations. Therefore, the more successful each one of them becomes, the more isolated he or she becomes from the original peer groups. The higher they go, the more isolated they become. Ultimately, considerable stress and duress ensue unless they learn how to effectively reassess their position and keep the M above the E instead of allowing it to fall below.

Position #3 is a perfect position if the person dies right after achieving. However, when we look closely at the position, we can readily see what the problem is. When the M and the E are on the same level, there can be no upward movement. Therefore, instead of moving on to greater heights, the person likes the current position and tends to focus his attention on staying at that level. However, what is not going up must come down. As he tries to hold his position on the B-D Scale, he will be in the process of failing.

Position #4 is the best position on the B-D Scale. That is because of the **proximity** of the M to the E and the **position** of the M in relation to the E. When the M is above the E and they are in close proximity, the chances for success are increased immeasurably. The M sort of serves as a magnet. It pulls the E. As the person achieves more, his aspirations also rise accordingly. Therefore, the more realistic the goals, the more likely they will be achieved.

The B-D Scale will help a person to realistically assess his current position in society, and it provides an opportunity for developing viable options. The next task is to help you find your position on the B-D Scale. Let us begin by reviewing the Point Value Scale.

POINT VALUE SCALE

Factor #1—Environment		
20 pts. max.		
A. Home Value	$1,000,000 or more	= 20 pts.
B. Home Value	$500,000–999,000	= 17 pts.
C. Home Value	$250,000–499,000	= 14 pts.
D. Home Value	$100,000–249,000	= 11 pts.
E. Home Value	$50,000–99,000	= 8 pts.
F. Home Value	$10,000–49,000	= 5 pts.
G. Home Value	Below 9,999	= 2 pts.

Factor #2—Health	
20 pts. max	
A. Excellent	= 20 pts.
B. Good	= 17 pts.
C. Fair	= 14 pts.
D. Poor	= 11 pts.

Factor #3—Wealth			
20 pts. max.			
Yearly Income:	A.	$1,000,000 or more	= 20 pts.
	B.	$500,000–999,000	= 17 pts.
	C.	$250,000–499,000	= 14 pts.
	D.	$100,000–249,000	= 11 pts.
	E.	$50,000–99,000	= 8 pts.
	F.	$10,000–49,000	= 5 pts.
	G.	Below 9,999	= 2 pts.

Factor #4—Sex	
20 pts. max	
A. Male	= 20 pts.
B. Female	= 17 pts.
C. Homosexual	= 14 pts.
D. Lesbian	= 11 pts.
E. Other	= 7 pts.

Factor #5—Race	
20 pts. max	
A. White	= 20 pts.
B. Asian	= 17 pts.
C. Hispanic	= 14 pts.
D. Black	= 11 pts.
E. Others	= 7 pts.

To determine your position on the B-D Scale simply take the following steps:

Step 1: Identify the point value from the Point Value Scale for each of the five factors listed.

Step 2: Total up your points. See example below.

Factors	Persons				
	A	B	C	D	E
1. Environment	14	20	17	5	11
2. Health	20	20	17	11	20
3. Wealth	11	17	11	5	8
4. Sex	20	17	14	20	20
5. Race	20	20	20	20	11
Total Points	85	94	80	60	70
Position on B-D Scale—Level	2	2	3	5	3

Person A—Home is worth $250,000; excellent health; makes $100,000 yearly; male; white.

Person B—Home is worth $1,000,000; excellent health; makes $500,000 yearly; female, black.

Person C—Home is worth $500,000; good health; makes $200,000 yearly; homosexual; white.

Person D—Home is worth $49,000; poor health; makes $35,000 yearly; male, white.

Person E—Home is worth $100,000; excellent health; makes $60,000 yearly; male; black.

Now find your position on the B-D Scale by reviewing B-D Scale #5.

* * * *

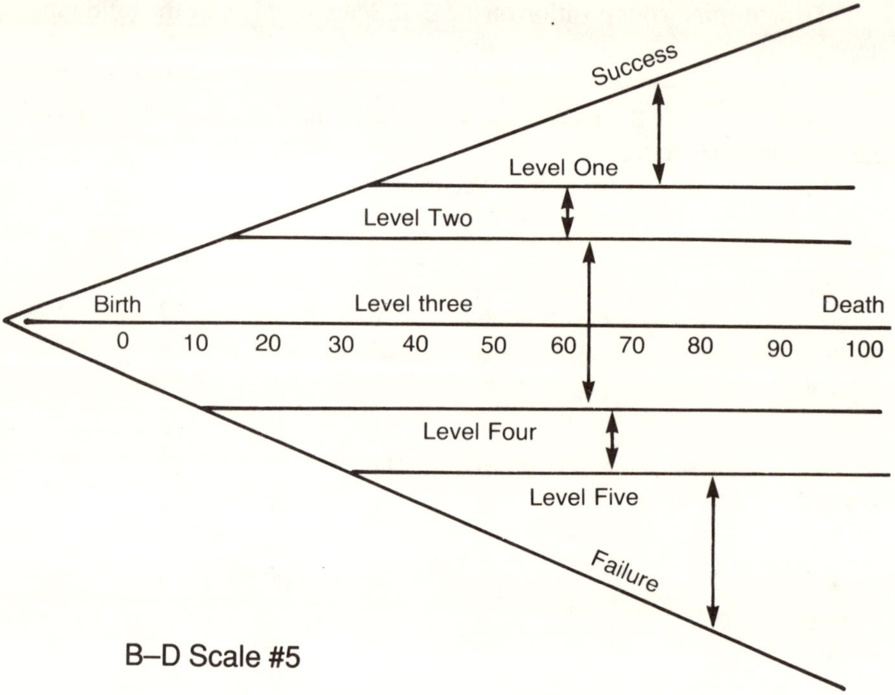

B–D Scale #5

Level One is the top position. The majority of the people on this level have enjoyed a long history of success, which has been passed down through generations.

Level Two is the second highest position. It is populated by people often referred to as the upper middle class. They are three to five generations removed from Level Three.

Level Three is the third highest position on the B-D Scale. It is populated by those who are called the middle class. This represents the largest segment of society. Over 50 percent of the population of the United States would fall within this category.

Level Four is the fourth highest position on the B-D Scale. It is populated by those who are three to four generations removed from Level Five. These people are often referred to as the lower middle class.

Level Five is the lowest position on the B-D Scale. People in this group are often referred to as the underclass or the poor. Most of them exist on some form of Welfare, and if they work, they possess menial, dirty, low-paying jobs. They are the last to be hired and the first to be fired.

Generally, people on Levels One through Four are motivated to succeed. Each of the four levels provides ample incentive and opportunities for upward mobility.

However, people on Level Five find fewer incentives and opportunities to motivate them to higher achievement. In fact, the opposite is true. Their environment and circumstances motivate them to perceive themselves as survivors. The tragedy is that they begin to think, feel, and behave like survivors on this level alone. They develop values and character traits which make it difficult or impossible for them to function effectively on the other four levels. For example, people on Level Five may develop the attitude that it is better to receive than it is to give. Their early negative conditioning and programming robs them of their childhood. Many young boys and girls, regardless of race, are forced into adulthood by incompetent parent models by age five. These children are forced into adult roles out of necessity. Parental neglect forces them to fend for themselves. Since they know little about the rules and values which govern larger society on the other levels, they develop their own. These, in many instances, tend to conflict significantly with the values and mores of larger society. Therefore, when persons on Level Five attempt to move to higher levels, they are not trained and emotionally equipped to deal with demands placed upon them at the higher levels. Their attitude and behavior become incongruent. This is one of the main reasons persons at Level Five appear to be permanently trapped at that level. In order for persons on Level Five to succeed, they must rid themselves of their particular type of survivor mentality. They have to be willing to make the sacrifice to develop a new outlook on themselves in particular and life in general. They must accept the fact that success has a high price, and they must be willing to pay the price.

They have to learn how to read, write, speak, and compute numbers effectively before they are in a position to take advantage of the opportunities for success which exist at the higher levels. They must also be flexible enough to identify those values they have which might mitigate against them achieving success at higher levels, and they must be willing to change, modify, or eliminate these values. In return, they must be willing to adopt new values which are congruent on respective levels. If this is done, many people who seem destined to remain on Level Five will be able to ultimately move to a higher level, one which is more commensurate with their skills, aptitudes, and interests.

The strategies for success which are outlined in this book will work well for a person functioning on any level. Person A and Person B both can substantially improve their success by understanding and applying the knowledge and principles delineated in this book.

The following table will help find your level on the B-D Scale.

B-D POSITION TABLE

Level	Points	Comparison with Assigned Population
Level 1	100–90	Approx. 2% of pop.
Level 2	89–80	Approx. 4% of pop.
Level 3	79–70	Approx. 54% of pop.
Level 4	69–60	Approx. 33% of pop.
Level 5	59 & below	Approx. 8% of pop.

So as you can see on the B-D Position Table that Level Five represents only a small percentage of the total population. However, it is still substantial in terms of numbers. Generally speaking, most of the persons categorized as A will be concentrated on the top four levels. Although it is possible for some Person A's to be on Level Five, it is highly unlikely. The next figure will help you see the correlation between the point value one has and the need level one would be functioning on according to Abraham Maslow's Hierarchy of Needs.

IMPACT OF POINT VALUES UPON MEETING HUMAN NEEDS

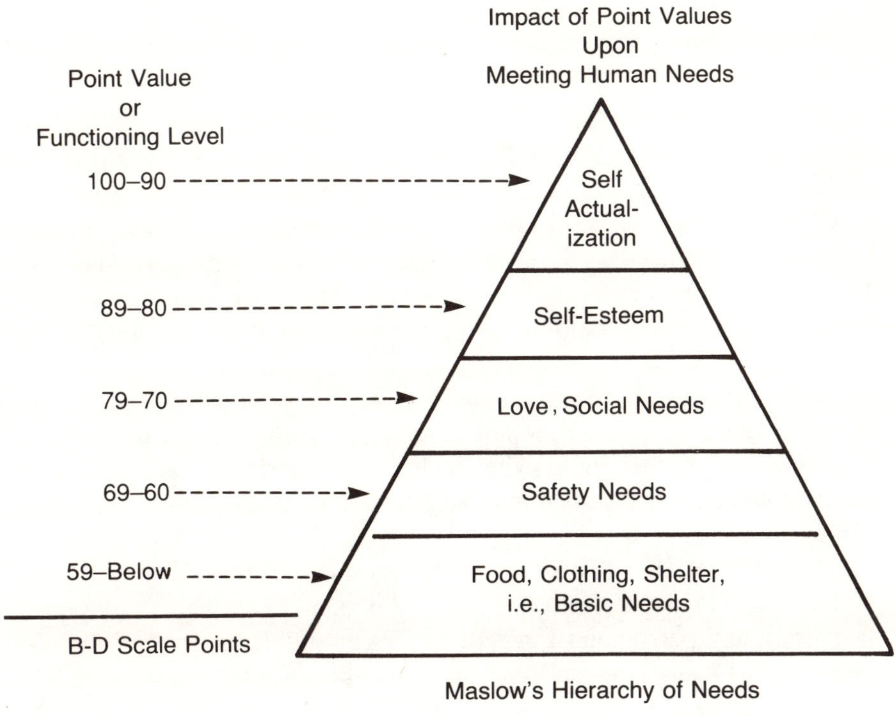

Level	Point Value or Functioning Level Points
1	100–90
2	89–80
3	79–70
4	69–60
5	59–Below

B-D Scale Points

This figure helps you see where the person is with respect to developing and utilizing his potential. Persons on Levels One, Two, and Three are doing an excellent job of meeting all of their needs. However, persons on Levels Four and Five are overburdened in trying to meet basic survival needs and safety needs. This is one of the most difficult groups to motivate, because the vast majority of their time is devoted to survival; therefore, the other needs appear to be of less importance to them. Consequently, they become acclimated to short-term goals instead of long-term goals. They have a burning desire to get as much out of life as they can. They tend to live from day to day, never preparing for a tomorrow, because they have no faith that tomorrow is going to be any better than today. Thus they become shortsighted and are totally unprepared to deal with emergencies when and if they appear.

The B-D Scale will also help persons on Levels One, Two, and Three better understand persons on Levels Four and Five. This is important because many persons on Levels One, Two, and Three tend to feel that persons on Levels Four and Five are there because they lack the will or desire to aspire to higher things in life. Therefore, they conclude that the primary reason persons stay on Levels Four and Five is because they are lazy and unmotivated. They fail to see the long-term effects of negative programming and the influence it has upon a person's ability to develop a "success" attitude.

The next part of this book deals with fifteen human needs. It will provide you with insights and strategies which can help you become more effective in your personal life, and it can also help you help others who may not have had the opportunity to read this book.

PART III

Strategies for Dealing Effectively with Human Needs

NEEDS WORKSHEET #1A: THE NEED TO BELONG

1. The need to belong is a very important human need. It is critical in helping to determine self-worth.

2. What are the consequences when we are able to meet this need?

   A. List at least three.

      1. ______________________________

      2. ______________________________

      3. ______________________________

3. What are the consequences when we fail to meet this need?

   B. List at least three.

      1. ______________________________

      2. ______________________________

      3. ______________________________

4. How do we correct this problem?

   C. List at least three things that can be done.

      1. ______________________________

      2. ______________________________

      3. ______________________________

NEEDS WORKSHEET #1B: THE NEED TO BELONG

Listed below are ten agree or disagree statements.

Statements	Check One Agree	Disagree
1. I would enjoy living in the world by myself.	_____	_____
2. If I am going to be successful, it will primarily be because of my personal efforts.	_____	_____
3. I think it is okay to put my need ahead of my family's needs.	_____	_____
4. It is easy for me to love myself, even if no one else does.	_____	_____
5. I feel it is better for a person to look out for himself rather than worry about someone else.	_____	_____
6. As long as I know who I am, I don't care who else does.	_____	_____
7. What I think is more important than what others think.	_____	_____
8. I feel the family usually makes unfair demands upon me.	_____	_____
9. It is okay with me if I have no friends.	_____	_____
10. I don't care whether my family loves me or not.	_____	_____

NEEDS WORKSHEET #1C: THE NEED TO BELONG

Answer Sheet to Ten Agree or Disagree Statements
Feedback Data

Agree

1. You tend to be a loner.
2. You accept responsibility for success.
3. You are selfish.
4. You are not being honest with yourself.
5. You are concerned mostly for yourself.
6. You are egotistical.
7. You are egotistical.
8. You tend to dislike responsibility.
9. You are probably lying.
10. You are probably lying.

Disagree

1. You tend to enjoy people.
2. You are depending on others for success.
3. You value family above self.
4. You recognize the importance of others.
5. You value the importance of others.
6. You value how others perceive you.
7. You recognize that others' thinking influences you.
8. You tend to accept responsibility.
9. You recognize the value of friends.
10. You value the love of your family.

PERSONAL PROFILE

A=Agree	D=Disagree
Positive Profile	Negative Profile
1. D	1. A
2. A	2. D
3. D	3. A
4. D	4. A
5. D	5. A
6. D	6. A
7. D	7. A
8. D	8. A
9. D	9. A
10. D	10. A

THE NEED TO BELONG

The need to belong is a very important human need. It is critical in helping to determine self-worth.

A. Consequences When Met:

- Facilitates personal identity.
- Promotes socialization and positive value.
- Helps to define goals.
- Promotes a sense of well-being.
- Increases the value of family.

B. Consequences When Not Met:

- Promotes the development of negative values.
- A person tends to isolate himself from others.
- A person tends to feel rejected and not needed.
- A person tends to devalue himself and life.
- Promotes the possibility of self-destructive behavior.

C. How to Meet the Need (When Dealing with Others):

- Accept the person for himself.
- Accept the person into the group.
- Acquaint the person with what is expected of group members.
- Teach the person the values that are essential for effective group assimilation.
- Make the group experience a positive one.
- Help the person develop the skills that are critical for establishing cohesive relationships in a group setting.

D. How to Meet the Need (When Dealing with Self):

- Recognize the value of effective group relationships.
- Understand that the survival of the group is valued more than the individual.
- Learn to utilize the group effectively to maximize personal potential.
- Remember that the group values action more than words.
- People tend to judge a book by its cover more often than by its content; however, a good cover can only be depended upon to get you over until one has had ample time to peep inside.
- Realize that you are judged by the company you keep or don't keep.
- Become more family- and group-oriented.

NEEDS WORKSHEET #2A: THE NEED TO BE BELIEVED

1. The need to be believed is critical in helping to establish a feeling of self-worth.

2. What are the consequences when we are able to need this need?

   A. List at least three.

      1. ____________________

      2. ____________________

      3. ____________________

3. What are the consequences when we fail to meet this need?

   B. List at least three.

      1. ____________________

      2. ____________________

      3. ____________________

4. How do we correct the problem?

   C. List at least three things that can be done.

      1. ____________________

      2. ____________________

      3. ____________________

NEEDS WORKSHEET #2B: THE NEED TO BE BELIEVED

Listed below are ten agree or disagree statements.

Statements	Check One Agree	Check One Disagree
1. I don't care whether or not anyone believes what I say.	_____	_____
2. As long as I know I am telling the truth, I feel okay.	_____	_____
3. If people won't believe me, then I feel it is okay not to believe them.	_____	_____
4. When I tell the truth, I expect others to believe me.	_____	_____
5. I feel that when people don't like you, they won't believe you.	_____	_____
6. I only lie when it is important.	_____	_____
7. People should not hold it against me if I am forced to lie.	_____	_____
8. Even if I have lied a lot, people still should believe me when I tell the truth.	_____	_____
9. If I try to tell the truth and no one believes me, it is okay not to try again.	_____	_____
10. If I lied and did not know I was lying, people should not hold it against me.	_____	_____

NEEDS WORKSHEET #2C: THE NEED TO BE BELIEVED

Answer Sheet to Ten Agree or Disagree Statements
Feedback Data

Agree

1. You are probably lying.
2. You are comfortable with your beliefs.
3. You believe in fair play.
4. You are very confident.
5. You are correct—they won't.
6. When is it not important?
7. You expect to lie.
8. You must be kidding.
9. No wonder you have a problem.
10. Wrong again; ignorance is no excuse.

Disagree

1. You recognize the value of others.
2. You are too dependent upon others.
3. You are overly dependent upon others.
4. You are unsure of yourself.
5. You have been misinformed about people.
6. People lie because they feel a need to.
7. People feel once a liar, always a liar.
8. People know who you are.
9. Lying should not be based on acceptance.
10. Ignorance does not justify lying.

PERSONAL PROFILE

A=Agree	D=Disagree
Positive Profile	Negative Profile
1. D	1. A
2. A	2. D
3. A	3. D
4. A	4. D
5. A	5. D
6. D	6. A
7. D	7. A
8. D	8. A
9. D	9. A
10. D	10. A

THE NEED TO BE BELIEVED

The need to be believed is critical in helping to establish a feeling of self-worth.

A. Consequences When Met:

- A person tends to feel better about himself.
- A person tends to feel better about others.
- A person tends to develop a more positive outlook on life.
- A person tends to develop a better appreciation about community values.
- A person tends to lie less frequently.

B. Consequences When Not Met:

- A person tends to feel rejected.
- A person sometimes tends to become hostile.
- A person tends to lie with impunity.
- It makes it more difficult for a person to achieve a positive status in the group.
- A person is more likely to devalue the group experience.

C. How to Meet the Need (When Dealing with Others):

- A person needs to be openly confronted when he is lying.
- A person needs to be taught the value of truth.
- It is important that a person feels that he is believed.
- Set a good example when dealing with this type of person.

D. How to Meet the Need (When Dealing with Self):

- Learn to value truth even when it is not to your personal advantage.
- Remember to share information without embellishing it.
- Sometimes it is easier to face the music than it is to rewrite the song.
- The more you tell the truth, the more others will believe you.
- The more others believe you, the better they tend to perceive you to be.

NEEDS WORKSHEET #3A: THE NEED TO BE ACCEPTED

1. The need to be accepted is extremely important in the socialization process.
2. What are the consequences when we are able to effectively meet this need?

   A. List at least three.

      1. ______________________________
      2. ______________________________
      3. ______________________________

3. What are the consequences when we fail to meet this need?

   B. List at least three.

      1. ______________________________
      2. ______________________________
      3. ______________________________

4. How do we correct this problem?

   C. List at least three things that can be done.

      1. ______________________________
      2. ______________________________
      3. ______________________________

NEEDS WORKSHEET #3B: THE NEED TO BE ACCEPTED

Listed below are ten agree or disagree statements.

Statements	Check One Agree	Disagree
1. I really don't care what people think of me.	_____	_____
2. It is more important that I accept me even if others do not.	_____	_____
3. When I dress, I dress to please myself, not others.	_____	_____
4. If people don't like me, then it is easy for me not to like them.	_____	_____
5. I feel good when others respect me.	_____	_____
6. I would rather be by myself than with a group of people.	_____	_____
7. I think it is better to receive than it is to have to give up something.	_____	_____
8. I feel I am as good as everyone else.	_____	_____
9. People tend to like you more when you stand on your own two feet.	_____	_____
10. People won't accept you if you are too smart.	_____	_____

NEEDS WORKSHEET #3C: THE NEED TO BE ACCEPTED

Answer Sheet To Ten Agree or Disagree Statements
Feedback Data

Agree

1. You are lying.
2. You are correct. How you feel counts.
3. You are lying again.
4. You are correct. Hate breeds hate.
5. Most people dislike rejection.
6. You may be a loner.
7. You are a parasite.
8. You probably are.
9. You like independence.
10. You are probably too arrogant.

Disagree

1. You recognize the value of others.
2. You are too dependent upon others.
3. You correctly recognize the value of others.
4. You have difficulty disliking others.
5. You do not like rejection.
6. You value the company of others.
7. You tend to be benevolent.
8. You probably aren't.
9. You like being dependent.
10. You recognize that people will accept you if you are smart.

PERSONAL PROFILE

A=Agree

Positive Profile

1. D
2. A
3. D
4. A
5. D
6. D
7. D
8. A
9. A
10. D

D=Disagree

Negative Profile

1. A
2. D
3. A
4. D
5. A
6. A
7. A
8. D
9. D
10. A

THE NEED TO BE ACCEPTED

The need to be accepted is extremely important in the socialization process.

A. Consequences When Met:

- A person tends to feel important.
- A person tends to behave as if he is important.
- A person tends to develop a higher sense of self-worth.
- A person is more likely to perpetuate the ideals of the group.
- A person is more likely to develop more of his potential.

B. Consequences When Not Met:

- A person tends to feel rejected.
- A person is more inclined to reject others.
- The person will not develop the values that are essential for effective group participation.
- A person is less likely to develop his full potential.
- A person is likely to devalue himself and others.
- A person often will fail to develop a sense of personal pride.
- A person tends to develop a distorted sense of history.

C. How to Meet the Need (When Dealing with Others):

- Let the person know that he is acceptable.
- Give unmistakable outward signs of acceptance such as a smile, a touch, et cetera.
- Praise a person for his efforts as well as for his accomplishments.
- Help a person feel that he can be himself and still be loved and accepted.
- Let a person know that you feel that he can be trusted.
- Listen to a person's opinions. Don't be too quick to reject or criticize his ideas.
- Reject the person's ideas, if you must, without rejecting the person.

D. How to Meet the Need (When Dealing with Self):

- It is important to learn to love yourself.
- Concentrate on your assets and not what others perceive as liabilities.
- Accept the fact that not everyone will accept your greatness.

- Develop a personality which will enhance your attributes.
- Become more knowledgeable about what is and is not acceptable behavior.
- Do not overreact to real or imagined slights.

NEEDS WORKSHEET #4A: THE NEED TO ACHIEVE

1. The need to achieve ranks high on the list of values viewed as essential for effective human interaction.
2. What are the consequences when we are able to meet this need?

   A. List at least three.

   1. ______________________________
   2. ______________________________
   3. ______________________________

3. What are the consequences when we fail to meet this need?

   B. List at least three.

   1. ______________________________
   2. ______________________________
   3. ______________________________

4. How do we correct this problem?

   C. List at least three things that can be done.

   1. ______________________________
   2. ______________________________
   3. ______________________________

NEEDS WORKSHEET #4B: THE NEED TO ACHIEVE

Listed below are ten agree or disagree statements

Statements	Check One Agree	Disagree
1. The harder a person works, the more he will achieve.	_____	_____
2. I feel it is more important to try than it is to succeed.	_____	_____
3. People overemphasize the importance of achievement.	_____	_____
4. I find it difficult to get excited about achievements.	_____	_____
5. The process of achievement is more valuable than the end product.	_____	_____
6. I feel great when I accomplish something worthwhile.	_____	_____
7. It is easier to be successful if you get all of the good breaks.	_____	_____
8. I tend to value those achievements which require the least amount of effort.	_____	_____
9. I feel it is easier to achieve when you are around successful people.	_____	_____
10. Success is not what it is made out to be.	_____	_____

NEEDS WORKSHEET #4C: THE NEED TO ACHIEVE

Answer Sheet to Ten Agree or Disagree Statements
Feedback Data

Agree

1. You believe hard work pays off.
2. You place your emphasis upon effort.
3. You tend to devalue achievement.
4. You are probably underachieving.
5. You probably have few achievements.
6. You are achievement-oriented.
7. You depend too much upon luck.
8. You are lazy.
9. Success breeds success.
10. Where have you been? On Mars?

Disagree

1. You recognize that hard work may not pay off.
2. You tend to emphasize output over effort.
3. You feel that achievement cannot be oversold.
4. You recognize the excitement of success.
5. You have the process in perspective.
6. You may lack confidence in your success.
7. You realize that you make your own breaks.
8. You realize the price of success.
9. You are running with the wrong crowd.
10. You recognize the value of success.

PERSONAL PROFILE

A=Agree

Positive Profile

1. A
2. A
3. D
4. D
5. D
6. A
7. D
8. D
9. A
10. D

D=Disagree

Negative Profile

1. D
2. D
3. A
4. A
5. A
6. D
7. A
8. A
9. D
10. A

THE NEED TO ACHIEVE

The need to achieve ranks high on the list of values viewed as essential for effective human interaction and functioning.

A. Consequences When Met:

- A person tends to value himself more.
- A person tends to value others more.
- It helps a person feel better about himself.
- A person tends to develop more of his latent potential.
- It increases the person's value to the group.
- A person is often energized by the recognition given for personal accomplishments.

B. Consequences When Not Met:

- A person tends to avoid challenges.
- A person tends to feel unworthy.
- Others tend to view the person negatively.
- A person fails to develop the confidence needed to realize his potential.
- A person tends to play down the importance of achievements.
- A person tends to stop trying, and often he gives up easily.
- A person tends to avoid situations which might be competitive.

C. How to Meet the Need (When Dealing with Others):

- A person should be taught the value of achievement.
- A person should be taught how to achieve.
- A person should be given tasks with a high probability of success.
- A person must learn that achievement has a price tag.
- A person should receive recognition for even modest accomplishments.

D. How to Meet the Need (When Dealing with Self):

- Understand that achievement is a by-product of effort.
- Recognize that the value of achievement may reside more in process than in the outcome.
- Become more achievement-oriented. Develop latent abilities and always eagerly look forward to new challenges and opportunities.

NEEDS WORKSHEET #5A: THE NEED TO BE RECOGNIZED

1. The need to be recognized is key in facilitating a sense of achievement and positive feeling about self.

2. What are the consequences when we are able to meet this need?

   A. List at least three.

      1.______________________________

      2.______________________________

      3.______________________________

3. What are the consequences when we fail to meet this need?

   B. List at least three.

      1.______________________________

      2.______________________________

      3.______________________________

4. How do we correct this problem?

   C. List at least three things that can be done.

      1.______________________________

      2.______________________________

      3.______________________________

NEEDS WORKSHEET #5B: THE NEED TO BE RECOGNIZED

Listed below are ten agree or disagree statements.

Statements	Check One Agree	Disagree
1. I have often let others take credit for something I had done.	_____	_____
2. Recognition is not necessary for me.	_____	_____
3. I feel uncomfortable when others congratulate me.	_____	_____
4. When in a classroom, I am always sitting in the back row.	_____	_____
5. I never raise my hand in any situation.	_____	_____
6. I try not to do things that call attention to myself.	_____	_____
7. People usually congratulate the wrong people.	_____	_____
8. I am often given recognition for my achievements.	_____	_____
9. No one seems to care about my achievements.	_____	_____
10. I feel recognition helps me to achieve more.	_____	_____

NEEDS WORKSHEET #5C: THE NEED TO BE RECOGNIZED

Answer Sheet to Ten Statements
Feedback Data

Agree

1. You lack self-confidence.
2. You have a low self-concept.
3. You tend to feel unworthy.
4. You don't like being seen.
5. You tend to be unsure of yourself.
6. You may have an inferiority complex.
7. You tend to feel overlooked.
8. You are probably a high achiever.
9. You probably haven't achieved much.
10. You are reinforced when you achieve.

Disagree

1. You take credit where it is due.
2. You recognize the value of recognition.
3. You take your success in stride.
4. You are not afraid of being up front.
5. You are confident and competent.
6. You probably crave the attention.
7. You make sure you are not overlooked.
8. Others tend to devalue your achievements.
9. You make sure you are recognized.
10. You probably feel unrewarded for your efforts.

PERSONAL PROFILE

A=Agree	D=Disagree
Positive Profile	Negative Profile
1. D	1. A
2. D	2. A
3. D	3. A
4. D	4. A
5. D	5. A
6. D	6. A
7. D	7. A
8. A	8. D
9. D	9. A
10. A	10. D

THE NEED TO BE RECOGNIZED

The need to be recognized is key in facilitating a sense of achievement and a positive feeling about self.

A. Consequences When Met:

- A person tends to feel appreciated by others.
- A person tends to have a greater appreciation for the achievements of others.
- A person is more likely to develop his latent potential.
- A person tends to develop values which often promote effective group participation.

B. Consequences When Not Met:

- A person tends to feel unappreciated for his effort.
- A person tends to withdraw from others.
- A person tends to embellish his accomplishments.
- A person sometimes develops bizarre behavior to call attention to himself.
- A person tends to discount the performance of others.
- A person can develop feelings of hostility.
- It can and does lead to the development of antisocial behavior.
- A person can become vindictive and angry.

C. How to Meet the Need (When Dealing with Others):

- It is important to understand the need for recognition and not overreact to it.
- It is important to laud others for their accomplishments.
- It is important to distinguish between the recognition.
- Do not become jealous or threatened by others' need for recognition.

D. How to Meet the Need (When Dealing with Self):

- Understand your own strengths and weaknesses.
- Realize that everyone will not applaud you for your skills and abilities.
- Learn to accept your attributes in a positive way.
- Do not apologize for your shortcomings. Accept them and others will, too.
- Learn to accept praise without overreacting.

NEEDS WORKSHEET #6A: THE NEED TO BE VALUED

1. The need to be valued is critical in helping a person to establish a positive sense of self-worth.
2. What are the consequences when we are able to meet this need?

   A. List at least three.

      1. ______________________________
      2. ______________________________
      3. ______________________________

3. What are the consequences when we fail to meet this need?

   B. List at least three.

      1. ______________________________
      2. ______________________________
      3. ______________________________

4. How do we correct this problem?

   C. List at least three things that can be done.

      1. ______________________________
      2. ______________________________
      3. ______________________________

NEEDS WORKSHEET #6B: THE NEED TO BE VALUED

Listed below are ten agree or disagree statements.

Statements	Check One: Agree	Disagree
1. Most of the time, I don't care what others think of me.	_____	_____
2. I have always been popular.	_____	_____
3. People generally say good things about me.	_____	_____
4. I feel I am just as good as anyone else.	_____	_____
5. Sometimes I have felt worthless.	_____	_____
6. I cannot change how people feel about me.	_____	_____
7. People often have said that I was no good.	_____	_____
8. I have always known who I am.	_____	_____
9. If I could be someone else, I would gladly change.	_____	_____
10. I would rather be rich than loved.	_____	_____

NEEDS WORKSHEET #6C: THE NEED TO BE VALUED

Answer Sheet to Ten Agree or Disagree Statements
Feedback Data

Agree

1. You are probably lying.
2. You are probably successful.
3. You probably are doing good things.
4. You probably are confident.
5. Most people experience that feeling.
6. You underestimate your power.
7. You probably earned the recognition.
8. You are unique if you have always known who you are.
9. You may not be satisfied.
10. You place a higher value on material things.

Disagree

1. You value what others think.
2. You may tend to be a loner.
3. What good things have you done?
4. You might lack self-confidence.
5. You probably have a bad memory.
6. You recognize that you influence others.
7. Others tend to view you positively.
8. Most of us spent time finding out.
9. You have accepted who you are.
10. You place a lower value on material things.

PERSONAL PROFILE

A=Agree	D=Disagree
Positive Profile	Negative Profile
1. D	1. A
2. A	2. D
3. A	3. D
4. A	4. D
5. A	5. D
6. D	6. A
7. D	7. A
8. D	8. A
9. D	9. A
10. D	10. A

THE NEED TO BE VALUED

The need to be valued is critical in helping a person to establish a positive sense of self-worth.

A. Consequences When Met:

- A person tends to feel wanted.
- A person tends to feel needed.
- A person tends to feel important.
- A person tends to take pride in his activities.
- A person tends to develop a stronger sense of community.
- A person tends to have a keener awareness of his potential.
- A person tends to value others more.

B. Consequences When Not Met:

- A person tends to feel worthless.
- A person tends to value others less.
- A person tends to feel shortchanged or cheated.
- It can cause a person to develop a negative outlook on life.
- A person tends to feel unloved and unlovable.
- A person tends to become antisocial.
- A person tends to withdraw from others.
- A person tends to develop values which prevent him from interacting effectively in social situations.

C. How to Meet the Need (When Dealing with Others):

- Let the person know that you feel he is important.
- Give the person some responsibilities which are commensurate with his abilities.
- Recognize the person's achievements.
- Praise him in the presence of others for his accomplishments.
- Minimize the person's deficiencies by stressing his strong points.

D. How to Meet the Need (When Dealing with Self):

- Learn to accept yourself for who you are.
- Understand that you are important.
- Let your deeds be consistent with your values.
- Recognize that others tend to value you as you value yourself.
- Learn to love yourself regardless of what your perceived deficits might be.
- Accept the fact that others may not value you regardless of your efforts to the contrary.

NEEDS WORKSHEET #7A: THE NEED TO BE UNDERSTOOD

1. The need to be understood is critical in promoting effective human functioning.

2. What are the consequences when we are able to meet this need?

   A. List at least three.

      1.____

      2.____

      3.____

3. What are the consequences when we fail to meet this need?

   B. List at least three.

      1.____

      2.____

      3.____

4. How do we correct this problem?

   C. List at least three things that can be done.

      1.____

      2.____

      3.____

NEEDS WORKSHEET #7B: THE NEED TO BE UNDERSTOOD

Listed below are ten agree or disagree statements.

Statements	Check One Agree	Disagree
1. I seldom have to repeat a statement.	_____	_____
2. Usually I am very clear and concise when communicating with others.	_____	_____
3. I always get excellent compliments on my communication skills.	_____	_____
4. I only talk when I am sure of myself.	_____	_____
5. People tend to value my opinions.	_____	_____
6. Some people have suggested that I improve my communication skills.	_____	_____
7. I get angry when people ask me to repeat myself.	_____	_____
8. Most people are not good listeners.	_____	_____
9. People don't listen to me because they don't think I am important.	_____	_____
10. Most of the time, I am a good listener.	_____	_____

NEEDS WORKSHEET #7C: THE NEED TO BE UNDERSTOOD

Answer Sheet to Ten Agree or Disagree Statements
Feedback Data

Agree

1. You are a very good communicator.
2. You have no problems communicating.
3. You are above average.
4. You don't talk much.
5. You probably give good advice.
6. They care about you.
7. You are a poor communicator.
8. Good observation.
9. You don't impress others.
10. You are attentive.

Disagree

1. Most of us have to repeat ourselves.
2. You may need to improve your communication skills.
3. You are average.
4. You are not afraid to make a mistake.
5. You need to evaluate your feedback.
6. Either you are excellent or they don't care.
7. You probably don't have to repeat yourself often.
8. You missed this one.
9. You recognize that there are other reasons why they don't listen.
10. You have difficulty focusing.

PERSONAL PROFILE

A=Agree	D=Disagree
Positive Profile	Negative Profile
1. A	1. D
2. A	2. D
3. A	3. D
4. D	4. A
5. A	5. D
6. A	6. D
7. D	7. A
8. A	8. D
9. D	9. A
10. A	10. D

THE NEED TO BE UNDERSTOOD

The need to be understood is critical in promoting effective human functioning.

A. Consequences When Met:

- A person tends to feel that his opinions have merit.
- It improves a person's ability to communicate.
- A person tends to feel a closer kinship to others.
- A person tends to become more receptive to feedback during the communication process.

B. Consequences When Not Met:

- A person tends to feel that others do not value his input.
- A person tends to communicate poorly.
- It can have a negative impact on a person's self-image.
- A person tends to misinterpret others.

C. How to Meet the Need (When Dealing with Others):

- Let a person know that he is understood by confirming his message.
- If a person has difficulty expressing his ideas or feelings be patient with him.
- Don't tell the person that he has a communications problem; help him to solve it.
- Make sure that your own ideas are clear and concise.

D. How to Meet the Need (When Dealing with Self):

- Learn to be more precise in presenting your ideas.
- Become a better listener.
- Obtain feedback on a timely basis to facilitate communications.
- Expand your ability to communicate by developing your communication skills.

NEEDS WORKSHEET #8A: THE NEED TO COMMUNICATE

1. The need to communicate is crucial to personal development and survival.
2. What are the consequences when we are able to meet this need?

   A. List at least three.

      1. ______________________________
      2. ______________________________
      3. ______________________________

3. What are the consequences when we fail to meet this need?

   B. List at least three.

      1. ______________________________
      2. ______________________________
      3. ______________________________

4. How do we correct this problem?

   C. List at least three things that can be done.

      1. ______________________________
      2. ______________________________
      3. ______________________________

NEEDS WORKSHEET #8B: THE NEED TO COMMUNICATE

Listed below are ten agree or disagree statements.

Statements	Check One Agree	Disagree
1. I have excellent verbal skills.	_____	_____
2. Writing has always been easy for me.	_____	_____
3. Seldom do I have to use a dictionary to look up a word for spelling.	_____	_____
4. Generally, I am at ease when communicating with others.	_____	_____
5. I really enjoy speaking before a large group.	_____	_____
6. I have no problem speaking out in difficult situations.	_____	_____
7. Often I find myself at a loss for words.	_____	_____
8. People have laughed at the way I talk.	_____	_____
9. Few opportunities have gotten by me because I failed to speak out.	_____	_____
10. If I am not sure of what a person says, I ask him to repeat it.	_____	_____

NEEDS WORKSHEET #8C: THE NEED TO COMMUNICATE

Answer Sheet to Ten Agree or Disagree Statements
Feedback Data

Agree

1. You have one of the tools for communication.
2. You have an excellent communication skill.
3. You have an extensive vocabulary.
4. You are very self-assured.
5. You have strong leadership potential.
6. You are very confident.
7. You have difficulty thinking under pressure.
8. You have a speech problem.
9. You are confident and aggressive.
10. You provide excellent feedback to others.

Disagree

1. You lack an important communication tool.
2. You lack an essential tool.
3. You are average—most people need it.
4. You have difficulty communicating with others.
5. You are not sure of your potential.
6. You are unsure of yourself.
7. You never have a problem with words.
8. You blend well with your peers.
9. You lack confidence in your ability to persuade others.
10. You provide poor feedback to others.

PERSONAL PROFILE

A=Agree	D=Disagree
Positive Profile	Negative Profile
1. A	1. D
2. A	2. D
3. A	3. D
4. A	4. D
5. A	5. D
6. A	6. D
7. D	7. A
8. D	8. A
9. A	9. D
10. A	10. D

NEEDS WORKSHEET #9A: THE NEED FOR STRUCTURE

1. The need for structure is extremely important in helping the person develop a sense of security.

2. What are the consequences when we are able to meet this need?

   A. List at least three.

   1. ______________________________
   2. ______________________________
   3. ______________________________

3. What are the consequences when we fail to meet this need?

   B. List at least three.

   1. ______________________________
   2. ______________________________
   3. ______________________________

4. How do we correct this problem?

   C. List at least three things that can be done.

   1. ______________________________
   2. ______________________________
   3. ______________________________

NEEDS WORKSHEET #9B: THE NEED FOR STRUCTURE

Listed below are ten agree or disagree statements.

Statements	Check One Agree	Disagree
1. I feel there is a reason for everything.	_____	_____
2. A person is better off when he learns to set limits.	_____	_____
3. I resent being told what to do all the time.	_____	_____
4. I get along a lot better when I don't know what the rules are.	_____	_____
5. I like to know where my next meal is coming from.	_____	_____
6. It is important for me to have things organized.	_____	_____
7. I always know where I put important things.	_____	_____
8. Usually I go to bed about the same time every night.	_____	_____
9. I really enjoy following a set routine.	_____	_____
10. I feel structure is important if one is going to predict outcomes.	_____	_____

NEEDS WORKSHEET #9C: THE NEED FOR STRUCTURE

Answer Sheet to Ten Agree or Disagree Statements
Feedback Data

Agree

1. You feel there is a cause and effect.
2. You have benefited from setting limits.
3. You dislike being regimented.
4. You feel confined by rules.
5. You dislike uncertainty.
6. You enjoy structure.
7. You are well organized.
8. You are a creature of habit.
9. You feel positive about discipline.
10. You are confident of your decision-making skills.

Disagree

1. You have refused to think about it.
2. You resent limits and probably most authorities.
3. You are probably easily manipulated.
4. You are uncomfortable without rules.
5. You are comfortable with uncertainty.
6. You dislike structure.
7. You can't find anything—nothing has a place.
8. You are totally disorganized.
9. You dislike the discipline structure requires.
10. You lack effective decision-making skills.

PERSONAL PROFILE

A=Agree	D=Disagree
Positive Profile	Negative Profile
1. A	1. D
2. A	2. D
3. A	3. D
4. D	4. A
5. A	5. D
6. A	6. D
7. A	7. D
8. A	8. D
9. A	9. D
10. A	10. D

THE NEED FOR STRUCTURE

The need for structure is extremely important in helping the person develop a sense of security and stability.

A. Consequences When Met:

- A person tends not to bite off more than he can chew.
- A person tends to learn the value of limits.
- A person tends to develop a better balance in his personal life.
- A person tends to develop more of his potential and abilities.
- A person tends to value structure more.

B. Consequences When Not Met:

- A person tends to ignore limits and often overextends himself.
- A person will sometimes exceed expectations.
- A person often experiences difficulty in setting realistic goals.
- A person tends to feel insecure about his environment.
- A person tends to resent the weight of responsibility.

C. How to Meet the Need (When Dealing with Others):

- Help the person learn the value of structure through experience.
- Demonstrate the benefits of setting realistic goals.
- Focus on the benefits of structure and not the confining aspects.

D. How to Meet the Need (When Dealing with Self):

- Understand the value of knowing limits.
- Be aware of the consequences of not imposing limitations on one's expectations.
- Also be aware of setting limits which might be too restrictive.
- Recognize your need for structure and be aware of any deficits.

NEEDS WORKSHEET #10A: THE NEED TO BE SATISFIED

1. The need to be satisfied is key in helping a person establish a sense of well-being.
2. What are the consequences when we are able to meet this need?

   A. List at least three.

   1. ______________________________
   2. ______________________________
   3. ______________________________

3. What are the consequences when we fail to meet this need?

   1. ______________________________
   2. ______________________________
   3. ______________________________

4. How do we correct this problem?

   1. ______________________________
   2. ______________________________
   3. ______________________________

NEEDS WORKSHEET #10B: THE NEED TO BE SATISFIED

Listed below are ten agree or disagree statements.

Statements	Check One: Agree	Check One: Disagree
1. I feel very good about myself.	_____	_____
2. Generally I am satisfied most of the time.	_____	_____
3. People often fail to appreciate my efforts.	_____	_____
4. Satisfaction is a fleeting, passing fancy.	_____	_____
5. It makes me feel very good when I achieve something worthwhile.	_____	_____
6. Regardless of what I do, I always feel it could have been done better.	_____	_____
7. It is much easier for me to satisfy myself than it is to satisfy others.	_____	_____
8. My satisfaction comes more from trying than from actually doing something well.	_____	_____
9. I believe that the moment a person is satisfied, he won't try to do better.	_____	_____
10. Dissatisfaction motivates me to work harder.	_____	_____

NEEDS WORKSHEET #10C: THE NEED TO BE SATISFIED

Answer Sheet to Ten Agree or Disagree Statements
Feedback Data

Agree	Disagree
1. You have a lot of self-confidence.	1. You lack self-confidence.
2. You are pleased with your performance.	2. You are unhappy with your performance.
3. You recognize that efforts are not always rewarded.	3. Your situation is exceptional.
4. You are unhappy with your outcomes.	4. You enjoy your results.
5. You are reinforced positively.	5. You are negatively reinforced.
6. You lack self-confidence.	6. You do not underrate your performance.
7. You're correct; satisfaction is personal.	7. You don't understand satisfaction.
8. You place your value on the "effort."	8. You place your value on the "outcome."
9. You feel satisfaction kills motivation.	9. You feel satisfaction does not effect motivation.
10. You are wrong. It demotivates you.	10. You recognize that dissatisfaction is a demotivator.

PERSONAL PROFILE

A=Agree	D=Disagree
Positive Profile	Negative Profile
1. A	1. D
2. A	2. D
3. A	3. D
4. D	4. A
5. A	5. D
6. D	6. A
7. A	7. D
8. D	8. A
9. D	9. A
10. D	10. A

THE NEED TO BE SATISFIED

The need to be satisfied is key in helping a person establish a sense of well-being.

A. Consequences When Met:

- A person tends to feel contented with his life.
- A person tends to get along better with others.
- A person tends to be more charitable.
- A person tends to view the future more positively.
- It tends to build a person's confidence.

B. Consequences When Not Met:

- A person appears to be unhappy most of the time.
- A person tends to doubt himself and others.
- A person tends to lose interest in life.
- A person tends to lose pride in personal accomplishments.
- A person may appear to be greedy and unconcerned about the welfare of others.
- A person may tend to discount his personal appearance.

C. How To Meet The Need (When Dealing with Others):

- Help the person feel good about himself.
- Reinforce the benefits of personal satisfaction.
- Help the person recognize satisfaction by identifying the feelings associated.

D. How to Meet the Need (When Dealing with Self):

- Learn to enjoy accomplishments.
- Fill your mind with positive thoughts upon task completion.
- Accept your accomplishments and achievements as your just rewards.
- Do not minimize the importance of your achievements.
- Remember that you are in charge of your feelings.

NEEDS WORKSHEET #11A: THE NEED TO BE ALONE

1. The need to be alone is important in helping a person to develop a higher sense of objectivity.
2. What are the consequences when we are able to meet this need?

   A. List at least three.

   1. ______________________________
   2. ______________________________
   3. ______________________________

3. What are the consequences when we fail to meet this need?

   B. List at least three.

   1. ______________________________
   2. ______________________________
   3. ______________________________

4. How do we correct this problem?

   C. List at least three things that can be done.

   1. ______________________________
   2. ______________________________
   3. ______________________________

NEEDS WORKSHEET #11B: THE NEED TO BE ALONE

Listed below are ten agree or disagree statements.

Statements	Check One Agree	Disagree
1. I believe that absence makes the heart grow fonder.	_____	_____
2. I feel everyone needs some time to themselves.	_____	_____
3. You can see things better when you have been gone awhile.	_____	_____
4. If you really love someone, you never want to be apart.	_____	_____
5. It is not good to be alone too often.	_____	_____
6. I feel more secure when I am alone.	_____	_____
7. It is not difficult for me to be alone even when I am in a crowd of people.	_____	_____
8. I get upset when others challenge my need to be alone.	_____	_____
9. It is difficult for me to say why I want to be alone.	_____	_____
10. People generally have no difficulty honoring my request to be alone.	_____	_____

NEEDS WORKSHEET #11C: THE NEED TO BE ALONE

Answer Sheet to Ten Agree or Disagree Statements
Feedback Data

Agree	Disagree
1. You value "free" time.	1. You dislike distance from significant others.
2. You enjoy being alone.	2. You are uncomfortable when alone.
3. You like objectivity.	3. You resent change.
4. You resent separation.	4. You welcome occasional separation.
5. You prefer the presence of others.	5. You enjoy being alone.
6. You are insecure with others.	6. You welcome the presence of others.
7. You know how to withdraw from others.	7. You are uncomfortable in a crowd.
8. You are not communicating effectively.	8. You recognize the possibility of conflict.
9. You have not examined your motives.	9. You know why you need to be alone.
10. You have not learned how to communicate your needs effectively.	10. You effectively communicate your needs.

PERSONAL PROFILE

A=Agree	D=Disagree
Positive Profile	Negative Profile
1. D	1. A
2. A	2. D
3. A	3. D
4. D	4. A
5. A	5. D
6. D	6. A
7. A	7. D
8. D	8. A
9. D	9. A
10. A	10. D

THE NEED TO BE ALONE

The need to be alone is important in helping a person to develop a higher sense of objectivity.

A. Consequences When Met:

- It permits a person time to regroup.
- It helps a person to more realistically assess a situation.
- It tends to increase the value of interpersonal relationships.
- It tends to improve a person's cognitive skills.
- It makes it easier to define issues.

B. Consequences When Not Met:

- A person can become hostile and resentful.
- A person tends to become withdrawn.
- A person tends to lose his objectivity.
- A person tends to feel suffocated.
- A person may become moody and uncooperative.

C. How to Meet the Need (When Dealing with Others):

- Give a person ample space.
- Respect his need for privacy.
- Do not feel personally rejected when space is requested.
- Let him know that you understand his need for space.
- Help him learn how to communicate this effectively.

D. How to Meet the Need (When Dealing with Self):

- Do not feel guilty about needing to be alone occasionally.
- Be open, and not secretive, about your need for space.
- Realize that others might resent or misinterpret your need for space.
- Do not wait until you are desperate before seeking escape to privacy.
- Recognize the need for privacy as legitimate.

NEEDS WORKSHEET #12A: THE NEED TO KNOW

1. The need to know is significant in facilitating a desire and quest for information.
2. What are the consequences when we are able to meet this need?

   A. List at least three.

      1. ____________________
      2. ____________________
      3. ____________________

3. What are the consequences when we fail to meet this need?

   B. List at least three.

      1. ____________________
      2. ____________________
      3. ____________________

4. How do we correct this problem?

   C. List at least three things that can be done.

      1. ____________________
      2. ____________________
      3. ____________________

NEEDS WORKSHEET #12B: THE NEED TO KNOW

Listed below are ten agree or disagree statements.

Statements	Check One Agree	Check One Disagree
1. Ignorance is bliss.	_____	_____
2. I feel I know all I need to know.	_____	_____
3. It is possible that you can know too much.	_____	_____
4. The less you know, the better off you are.	_____	_____
5. What you don't know can't hurt you.	_____	_____
6. No one likes a person who seems to know too much.	_____	_____
7. It is more important to know where to get the answer than it is to know the answer.	_____	_____
8. The more I learn, the more I learn I need to learn.	_____	_____
9. You learn more from observing than you do from active participation.	_____	_____
10. Book learning is okay, but experience is the best teacher.	_____	_____

NEEDS WORKSHEET #12C: THE NEED TO KNOW

Answer Sheet to Ten Agree or Disagree Statements
Feedback Data

Agree	Disagree
1. You must be ignorant.	1. Stupidity has no rewards.
2. You are content knowing nothing.	2. You recognize your informational gaps.
3. You have to be kidding.	3. It's not likely to happen.
4. You must like being well-off.	4. You realize this statement is ridiculous.
5. You have your head in the sand often.	5. Lack of knowledge is fatal.
6. You resent a show-off.	6. You must be a show-off.
7. You blew it.	7. You have the answer.
8. You missed the point again.	8. You are on your way to learning.
9. You are discounting the value of experience.	9. Active learning beats passive learning.
10. You place too much emphasis upon experience.	10. You recognize the need for both.

PERSONAL PROFILE

A=Agree	D=Disagree
Positive Profile	Negative Profile
1. D	1. A
2. D	2. A
3. D	3. A
4. D	4. A
5. D	5. A
6. A	6. D
7. A	7. D
8. A	8. D
9. D	9. A
10. D	10. A

THE NEED TO KNOW

The need to know is significant in facilitating a quest for information.

A. Consequences When Met:

- A person tends to become better informed.
- A person tends to make informed decisions.
- A person tends to take advantage of more opportunities.
- A person tends to develop more of his potential.

B. Consequences When Not Met:

- The less a person knows, the less he feels he needs to know.
- A person is less aware of viable options.
- A person is a poor problem solver.
- A person tends to be easily persuaded by the opinions of others.
- A person tends to have a restricted interest level.
- A person generally will not develop his potential.
- A person is easily victimized when confronted with anger and frustration.

C. How to Meet the Need (When Dealing with Others):

- Excite the person about the value of information.
- Expose the person to interesting and exciting data.
- Assist the person in the development of skills which are essential in the acquiring of data.
- Acclimate the person to the consequences of inadequate information.

D. How to Meet the Need (When Dealing with Self):

- Lean to enjoy data gathering.
- Develop your natural curiosity.
- Expand your ability to assimilate data.
- Remove any barriers which might prevent you from developing your talents.
- Remember the price one pays for an insufficient data base.

NEEDS WORKSHEET #13A: THE NEED TO COMPETE

1. The need to compete is essential in helping the person develop positive, aggressive feelings crucial for personal development.

2. What are the consequences when we are able to meet this need?

   A. List at least three.

      1. ____

      2. ____

      3. ____

3. What are the consequences when we fail to meet this need?

   B. List at least three.

      1. ____

      2. ____

      3. ____

4. How do we correct this problem?

   C. List at least three things that can be done.

      1. ____

      2. ____

      3. ____

NEEDS WORKSHEET #13B: THE NEED TO COMPETE

Listed below are ten agree or disagree statements.

Statements	Check One Agree	Disagree
1. Competition is for the birds.	_____	_____
2. I try to avoid competition whenever I can.	_____	_____
3. Competition is something men do to prove their manhood.	_____	_____
4. Competition tends to bring out the worst in people.	_____	_____
5. People will do anything to win.	_____	_____
6. There is no honor for the loser.	_____	_____
7. I feel competition is key in a democratic society.	_____	_____
8. Competitive people tend to think that they are always right.	_____	_____
9. Competition is barbaric. It is like the survival of the fittest.	_____	_____
10. Competition tends to build leadership and character.	_____	_____

NEEDS WORKSHEET #13C: THE NEED TO COMPETE

Answer Sheet to Ten Agree or Disagree Statements
Feedback Data

Agree	Disagree
1. You resent competition.	1. You value competition.
2. You are afraid to compete.	2. You enjoy competition.
3. You feel it is gender-oriented.	3. You recognize the need in male and female.
4. You view it negatively.	4. You recognize the positive aspects.
5. You don't trust people.	5. You believe people will compete fairly.
6. You place a negative value on losing.	6. You believe there is value in losing.
7. You are well-informed.	7. You must be from another planet.
8. You don't like competitive people.	8. You are not at odds with competition.
9. You are blinded by the effects of competition.	9. You perceive the positive benefits of competition.
10. You recognize the real value of competition.	10. You are not sure you can compete effectively.

PERSONAL PROFILE

A=Agree
Positive Profile
1. D
2. D
3. D
4. D
5. D
6. D
7. A
8. D
9. D
10. A

D=Disagree
Negative Profile
1. A
2. A
3. A
4. A
5. A
6. A
7. D
8. A
9. A
10. D

THE NEED TO COMPETE

The need to compete is essential in helping the person develop positive aggressive feelings crucial for personal development.

A. Consequences When Met:

- A person tends to feel more comfortable with challenges.
- It promotes healthy ego development.
- A person is forced to learn the rules of acceptable competitive behavior.
- It increases a person's aggressiveness.
- A person tends to develop more of his potential.
- It facilitates the development of leadership skills.

B. Consequences When Not Met:

- A person tends to withdraw from most competitive situations.
- A person tends to feel inadequate in situations which require open aggression.
- A person sometimes feels anger and inner directed hostility because of his perceived inadequacies.
- A person will deliberately avoid any competitive situation.
- If the person is a male, he is often perceived as being "less than a man."

C. How to Meet the Need (When Dealing with Others):

- Teach the person the value of open competition.
- Build the person's confidence in his ability to compete by involving him in competitive exercises commensurate with his aptitude, interests, and abilities.
- Help the person experience the "winning" feeling.
- Help the person identify his personal strengths and weaknesses.

D. How to Meet the Need (When Dealing with Self):

- Learn the value of competition.
- Understand the importance of competition and character development.
- Participate in activities which will help maximize your talents and abilities.
- Be honest with yourself. Admit it when you are in over your head.
- The key to success is competition and hard work. Be prepared to pay the price.

NEEDS WORKSHEET #14A: THE NEED TO COMPARE

1. The need to compare is key in helping a person to effectively discern differences.

2. What are the consequences when we are able to meet this need?

   A. List at least three.

      1. ______________________________

      2. ______________________________

      3. ______________________________

3. What are the consequences when we fail to meet this need?

   B. List at least three.

      1. ______________________________

      2. ______________________________

      3. ______________________________

4. How do we correct this problem?

   C. List at least three things that can be done.

      1. ______________________________

      2. ______________________________

      3. ______________________________

NEEDS WORKSHEET #14B: THE NEED TO COMPARE

Listed below are ten agree or disagree statements.

Statements	Check One Agree	Disagree
1. Differences tend to separate people.	_____	_____
2. It is important to be discriminating in one's judgment.	_____	_____
3. I feel people are just naturally drawn to opposites.	_____	_____
4. The grass always appears greener on the other side.	_____	_____
5. I wish I were taller.	_____	_____
6. You are not a good shopper if you don't do comparison shopping.	_____	_____
7. Comparing expands your knowledge base.	_____	_____
8. Sometimes I feel it is unfair to make comparisons.	_____	_____
9. Many times comparison makes a person feel inadequate.	_____	_____
10. I feel comfortable knowing where I really stand among my peers.	_____	_____

NEEDS WORKSHEET #14C: THE NEED TO COMPARE

Answer Sheet to Ten Agree or Disagree Statements
Feedback Data

Agree

1. You are observant.
2. You are knowledgeable.
3. You are a victim of misinformation.
4. Many agree with you.
5. You don't like your height.
6. You have benefitted from the experience.
7. You recognize the potential.
8. Comparisons can be unfair.
9. Only because of improper use.
10. You have been favorably compared with your peer group.

Disagree

1. Where have you been?
2. You missed this one.
3. You recognize that the statement is false.
4. You are in a minority.
5. You accept your height.
6. You are not a good shopper.
7. How could you miss this one?
8. You fail to see the negative side.
9. Properly used, comparisons are great.
10. You do not stack up well with your peers.

PERSONAL PROFILE

A=Agree	D=Disagree
Positive Profile	Negative Profile
1. A	1. D
2. A	2. D
3. D	3. A
4. D	4. A
5. D	5. A
6. A	6. D
7. A	7. D
8. A	8. D
9. A	9. D
10. A	10. D

THE NEED TO COMPARE

The need to compare is key in helping a person to effectively discern differences.

A. Consequences When Met:

- A person tends to sharpen his cognitive skills.
- A person tends to feel better about himself.
- A person tends to broaden his information base.
- A person tends to develop more of his abilities and potential.
- A person tends to develop a broader understanding of issues.
- It facilitates the development of leadership skills.

B. Consequences When Not Met:

- A person tends to have difficulty dealing with simple issues.
- A person is easily manipulated.
- A person tends to often be in a state of confusion.
- A person fails to fully develop his ability and potential.
- A person is not usually held in high esteem by his peers.
- It can retard a person's social development.

C. How to Meet the Need (When Dealing with Others):

- Help the person understand the value of the need to compare.
- Demonstrate the skills and techniques that may be used for making effective comparisons.
- Emphasize the value of effective discrimination.
- Affirm its value in the acquisition of knowledge and skills.
- Acclimate the person to its value in decision making and goal setting.

D. How to Meet the Need (When Dealing with Self):

- Learn that the ability to compare makes you more objective in your observations.
- It will help you increase your knowledge and understanding of your environment.
- Use the knowledge that accrues for positive reasons.
- Learn to appreciate and value differences.

NEEDS WORKSHEET #15A: THE NEED TO BELIEVE

1. The need to believe is key in motivating a person to cope with situations that require knowledge and skills beyond his experience.

2. What are the consequences when we are able to meet this need?

   A. List at least three.

      1. ____________________
      2. ____________________
      3. ____________________

3. What are the consequences when we fail to meet this need?

   B. List at least three.

      1. ____________________
      2. ____________________
      3. ____________________

4. How do we correct this problem?

   C. List at least three things that can be done.

      1. ____________________
      2. ____________________
      3. ____________________

NEEDS WORKSHEET #15B: THE NEED TO BELIEVE

Listed below are ten agree or disagree statements.

Statements	Check One Agree	Disagree
1. People have a need to believe.	_____	_____
2. Belief can help people overcome many obstacles.	_____	_____
3. Belief builds a person's confidence.	_____	_____
4. I would rather deal with facts than deal with beliefs.	_____	_____
5. Facts are more motivating than beliefs.	_____	_____
6. People who believe can manage their personal lives better.	_____	_____
7. People who believe tend to place a higher value on life.	_____	_____
8. Belief can help a person realize his full potential.	_____	_____
9. Beliefs are based on feelings, not fact.	_____	_____
10. Belief can't overcome everything.	_____	_____

NEEDS WORKSHEET #15C: THE NEED TO BELIEVE

Answer Sheet to Ten Agree or Disagree Statements
Feedback Data

Agree	Disagree
1. You recognize a well-known truth.	1. You believe you don't believe.
2. You understand the power of belief.	2. You do not know the power of belief.
3. You understand how it works in others.	3. You fail to believe its value.
4. You feel facts are more important.	4. You feel belief is more important.
5. You are misinformed on the facts.	5. You recognize the limitations about facts.
6. You understand the value of belief.	6. You are unfamiliar with the benefits of belief.
7. You recognize a key benefit of belief.	7. You fail to grasp the concept.
8. You realize belief makes it possible.	8. You have not been a beneficiary of belief.
9. You understand the difference.	9. You are unfamiliar with the difference.
10. You recognize limitations.	10. You fail to recognize limitations.

PERSONAL PROFILE

A=Agree	D=Disagree
Positive Profile	Negative Profile
1. A	1. D
2. A	2. D
3. A	3. D
4. D	4. A
5. D	5. A
6. A	6. D
7. A	7. D
8. A	8. D
9. A	9. D
10. A	10. D

THE NEED TO BELIEVE

The need to believe is key in motivating a person to cope with situations that require knowledge and skills beyond his experience.

A. Consequences When Met:

- A person feels capable of achieving the impossible.
- A person tends to overcome obstacles more easily.
- It makes the person feel more secure about himself.
- A person seems to enjoy life more.
- A person tends to value other persons more.
- It facilitates a stronger sense of community.

B. Consequences When Not Met:

- A person tends to have less confidence.
- A person tends to give up more easily when confronted with a difficult situation or task.
- A person tends to value his life less.
- A person tends to reject things that are unfamiliar.
- A person tends to be more ME-oriented.

C. How to Meet the Need (When Dealing with Others):

- Acclimate the person to the importance of belief.
- Lead more by example than by words.
- Help the person experience the value of belief.
- Recognize the fact that the need to believe is universal among humans.

D. How to Meet the Need (When Dealing with Self):

- Recognize the need in yourself.
- Understand the power of belief.
- Share your confidence with others.
- Use your knowledge of the power of belief to help others as well as yourself.
- Use your knowledge to develop your full potential.

PART IV

Motivational Strategies

There are three primary forms of motivation which warrant our attention. Motivation is often defined as the cause or reason for action.

SOURCE #1: FEAR. Fear is probably one of the most utilized forms of motivations. That is because it is simple and effective. It does not require much thought. In fact, it probably involves no thought relative to the consequences which might ensue.

There are several negative spin-offs which accrue from fear motivation. They are:

1. It is short-term.
2. It creates negative feelings.
3. It tends to be overused because of its simplicity.

So it quickly becomes obvious that the use of fear motivation is in the best interest of neither the person using it nor the person it is directed toward. People on Level Five of the B-D Scale use this form more than people on Levels One through Four. The reason is that it is often employed by a person who is constantly frustrated and in an agitated state of mind. Because of the difficulty people on Level Five encounter, they are continually angry and short-tempered.

SOURCE #2: INCENTIVE. Incentive is another well-known and broadly used form of motivation. Incentive motivation means that a reward, internal or external, is employed to motivate the individual. Incentive motivation works very well, except that at some point it begins to lose its value. For example, if one increases the incentive, it is highly unlikely that there will be a corresponding increase in productivity. In fact, in many instances, the opposite occurs, especially if the person feels that the additional incentive is inadequate, and he is likely to perform at a lower level than he was performing at before the additional incentive was added. There are also several negative spin-offs to incentive motivation. They are:

1. It does not increase productivity.
2. It too is short-term.
3. It is controlled by outside sources.

This does not mean that incentive motivation doesn't work, but it does mean that when one utilizes it, he should be aware of its shortcomings.

People on all five levels use this form of motivation regularly. It has won widespread use in our society.

SOURCE #3: ATTITUDINAL. Attitudinal is the third form of motivation I am going to share with you. Attitudinal motivation means the person is moved to action because he feels it is the right thing to do. In other words, the motivation stems from inside the person. Attitudinal motivation is the only form of motivation that provides unlimited opportunity. When a person is inner-directed, nothing prevents him from achieving his objectives. It helps the person overcome insurmountable obstacles. For example, there was the case of a lady who had a pickup truck run over her son in her driveway. This lady, even though she weighed less than 110 pounds, lifted the truck off her son! The story made the national news. Where did she get the strength? She was able to pick up that truck because she was inner-directed. She never stopped to see how heavy the truck was, nor did she assess her chances of lifting it. She felt the job had to be done and that she was the person to do it. Attitudinal motivation will help you achieve anything your mind can perceive.

TEN STEPS FOR BECOMING A MORE SUCCESSFUL PERSON

1. Know your B-D life position on the B-D Scale. Understand the implications of being programmed to succeed or fail. A person tends to adapt successfully to both positions. Remember that a person can consciously intervene and change either position.

2. When attempting to solve any problem, do not forget the steps in the decision-making process. First you must *think.* Reflect objectively and subjectively on the issues presented. Second, you must weigh the issues carefully or *reason* or rationally assess their relative value. Third, you must organize the consequences of *thinking and reasoning* into a body of information called knowledge and be prepared to utilize it to your advantage.

3. You must remember that all knowledge can be essentially broken down into two bodies of information: *empirical* and *metaphysical.* Empirical knowledge exists in the outer or objective world. You see, test, weigh, and measure empirical knowledge. It comprises what is commonly referred to as the "real world" or a body of facts. Metaphysical knowledge is compiled in the subjective world. It consists of all the information that is subjectively ascertained by you. It includes feelings, values, opinions, beliefs, colors, truths, politics, and religion. It cannot be objectively validated. You are the sole validating agent of all metaphysical knowledge.

4. Remember that metaphysical knowledge is more powerful than empirical knowledge. Beliefs are more important than facts.

5. It is difficult to discern when you are viewing issues empirically and when metaphysically. If strong emotions are involved, you are more than likely operating on a metaphysical level and your objectivity will be materially affected.

6. The more knowledgeable you are, the more comfortable you will be in utilizing empirical and metaphysical knowledge. It will help you to substantially improve your personal success.

7. When confronted with a problem, view it empirically and metaphysically. Ask yourself, "What are the facts?" Then ask what consequences are the most desirable. Always ask how much your feelings may be affecting your objectivity.

8. Learn to trust your judgment. As your decisions begin to produce more desirable outcomes, your confidence will improve correspondingly.

9. Make a commitment for personal development. The more you develop yourself, the greater the rewards. Remember, most successful people only use a small part of their potential. The Chain of Success depicted below will show you how to maximize job success:

CHAIN OF SUCCESS

ATTENDANCE	(Goal should be 100 percent.)
PUNCTUALITY	(Goal should be 100 percent. Be on time.)
ATTITUDE	(Get along well with others. Think and act positive.)
MOTIVATION	(Be energetic and tackle tasks enthusiastically.)
KNOWLEDGE	(Develop the necessary knowledge and skills for improving job performance.)

10. Remember the fifteen human needs. Review where you are in respect to meeting your needs. Also remember that there are often negative consequences when you fail to deal effectively with certain needs. Denying their existence can only be counterproductive. Do not procrastinate. Handle the negative consequences immediately.

SUGGESTED READINGS

BEHAVIOR MODIFICATION

Fensterhein, H. *Assertiveness Training Can Change Your Life: Don't Say Yes When You Want to Say No*. New York: McKay, 1975.

Kennedy, Eugene Cullen. *Believing*. New York: Doubleday, 1974.

Lazarus, Arnold A. *In the Mind's Eye: The Power of Imagery for Personal Enrichment*, 1st. ed. New York: Rowson Associates, 1977.

Redd, William H. *Personal Guide to Behavioral Modification*. New York: Random House, 1976.

Sartre, Jean-Paul. *Being and Nothingness*. New York: Philosophical Library, 1956.

Schrag, Peter. *Mind Control*. Pantheon, 1976.

Skinner, Burrhus F. *Beyond Freedom and Dignity*. New York: Knopf, 1971.

Smith, Manual J. *Kicking the Fear Habit*. New York: Dial Press, 1977.

MOTIVATION

Burke, Kenneth. *Permanence in Change*. Indianapolis: Babbs, 1965.

Gellerman, Saul W. *Management by Motivation*. New York: American Management Association, 1968.

Kunjufu, Jawnza. *Motivating and Preparing Black Youth to Work*. Chicago: African American Images, 1986.

Simon, Sidney B. *Value Clarification: A Handbook of Practical Strategies for Teachers and Students*. New York: Dodd, Mead, 1985.

Wellington, Charles Burleigh. *The Underachievers*. Chicago: Rand McNally, 1965.